THE

HISTORY AND DESCRIPTION

OF THE

SHETLAND ISLANDS;

WITH AN ACCOUNT OF THE

MANNERS, CUSTOMS, CIRCUMSTANCES, SUPERSTITIONS, AND RELIGION OF THE INHABITANTS.

BY THE REV. JAMES CATTON.

WHO WAS THREE YEARS

A WESLEYAN MISSIONARY IN SHETLAND.

PREFACE.

THE History and Description of the Shetland Islands will be found to contain matter of more general interest, than many persons would suppose, from their small importance and remote situation.

The Work will contain may things that will gratify the ANTIQUARIAN and the GEOLOGIST, the HISTORIAN and the PHILANTHROPHIST:—But it will be found principally suited to the simple enquirer after a knowledge of the most Northern Islands of the Empire, with the civil and religious condition of the Inhabitants.

The Work will comprise Three Parts.—The First will contain the History and Description of the Islands ; when they were discovered ; and by whom, at various times they have been inhabited; with an account of their Ancient Religion, Superstitions, Laws, &c.

The different Governors and Governments, under which the Islands have been placed.—The remarkable events which have taken place, connected with General History.—An account of the introduction of Christianity, into the Islands, by Olaus, the 1st King of Denmark, and when the Islands were transferred from Denmark to Scotland.—The present state and Political importance of the Islands,—Their Exports and Imports.

The Second Part will give a Description of the Islands.—The Number.—Geographical Situation, with the remarkable Promotories, Mountains, Natural Curiosities, Ancient Castles.—A Description of Lerwick, the Capital,—Harbours, Fishing Stations, Peculiarity of the Climate, and Natural History of the Islands, &c.

The Third Part will give an account of the Lairds, Peasantry, Merchants, Manners, Customs, Employment, and Poverty of the Inhabitants.

The Author does not aim at Elegance of Style, or any of the refinements of Composition, but with simplicity, aims only at correctness of Facts and Descriptions.

I have aimed at conciseness, as my object was to write a cheap little work as a 'vade mecum' for those who wish to travel through the Islands; and to give those at a distance, a general view, who have not leisure for reading a more lengthy and elaborate account.

Dr. Clarke intended, if his life had been spared, to have published a work on the Islands, a few fragments of which, with the correspondence between himself and the Missionaries, is now published in the last volume of his works.

I delayed publishing my work when I heard of something being likely to come forth on the subject in his Posthumous works; but finding, that what he had written did not at all militate against my work, I with diffidence and humility offer it to the Public.

Wainfleet, September 3rd, 1838.

PART THE FIRST.

HISTORY OF THE SHETLAND ISLANDS.

MANY things in ancient history are uncertain, and many things are fabulous, and popular traditions are so wrapped in mist and obscurity, that it is difficult to determine what is true, or what is ficticious, or what is a mixture of both.

These remarks are strikingly illustrated in the early history of these Islands; for tradition says, when the Romans visited them they were struck with their fertility and beauty, being covered over with large and beautiful trees, and that they set fire to them and burned them down to the ground, because these woods were a covert for the pirates and their plunder.

That these Islands were known to the Romans is, I think, beyond doubt, but it is very doubtful whether they were ever covered with trees. Some favour this tradition because of the great quantity of Peat which abounds here, which is generally allowed to be a decomposition of ligneous matter, and from the remains of trees found in the bogs; but these may be the relics of the deluge. For when we consider their present sterility and that of the adjacent Islands, and the total failure of every effort to get trees to grow unless sheltered by walls, the tradition is very doubtful.

That these Islands were known very early to the Romans appears evident from Virgil's Georgics, where in his Panegyric to Cæsar, he says

> Or over boundless ocean wilt thou reign,
> Smooth the wild billows of the roaring main,
> While utmost THULE shall thy nod obey.
>
> > Geor. 1st, 41st line.

But Eutropius and Orisius inform us, that the Emperor Claudius discovered the *Orcades*, which terms are supposed to be the general term for both Orkney and Shetland.

B

But Tacitus says, the Shetland Islands were not discovered until the year A. D. 85, the 4th of Domition, by Agricola.

It is most likely that the Orkneys, being much nearer Scotland, were discovered by Claudius, and that it was not until Agricola circumnavigated Britain, that the Shetlands were discovered; or at least it was not until then they were particularly mentioned or distinguished as a more distant and distinct group of Islands than the Orkneys.

He thus describes them, " Dispecta est et Thule quam nectemus nix et hiems ab debat," which represents, " Thule, which hitherto eternal snows and gloomy winter had concealed, was discovered."

The first persons who inhabited these Islands were most probably the pirates, who infested the North Seas, and who were led to make here a temporary abode, perhaps, more from necessity than choice. They were called the Sea Kings: they were Saxons and Danes.

The Danes and Saxons seem to have been of the same stock. They inhabited the peninsular of Jutland, the Isles of the Baltic, and the shores of the Scandinavian continent; there is an affinity in their language and similarity of profession.

In spring it was their custom to assail some distant province, and after ravaging the country and collecting the spoil to retire to some place of secrecy; so audacious at length became these depredators that the Romans found it necessary to exert themselves effectually against them.

Theodius is said to have chased them into their secret and remote haunts, which were *Orkney* and *Shetland*, and bedewed these Islands with their blood. *This event* took place in A. D. 369. To whose praise Claudian wrote, " Maduerunt Saxone fuso Orcades *incaluit Pictorum* Sanguine Thule." (*i.e.*) " The Orkneys were wet with the slaughter of the Saxons, and *Thule* became hot with the blood of the Picts."

This quotation from *Claudian* is greatly in favour of the Romans having been in Shetland; and proves also that the Picts at this period had either united with the Saxons in piratical enterprize, or, having become inhabitants of these Islands, they were taken to be pirates, and the innocent fell with the guilty.

It is certain, however, that the Picts were the first regular inhabitants both of Orkney and Shetland.

The Encyclopedia Perthensis considers that Pentland firth was so called as it was the firth entering Pictland or Pict's-land; and there are now in the Islands many ruins called Picts Castles, and Pict's houses. There are also many traditions in the Islands concerning the Picts.

Skinner in his Ecclesiastical History says, we have a cloud of concurring authorities that Palladius, the first bishop of the Scots, died and was buried in Terra Pictorium, among whom he had introduced Christianity. His death took place about the year A.D. 450. Boice says, Paladius ordained *Servanus*, whom he appointed to the Orkneys, and likewise made *Tervanus*, whom he had baptized when a child, Archbishop of the Picts.

Usher also says, St. Columba entreated King Brude, who was a Pictish king, to command the Prince of the Orkneys to be favourable to the Monks or Pappa, whom Columba had sent to these Islands—the truth of this statement is confirmed by this fact, that the two Islands of the Shetland group are called Pappa Little and Pappa Stour.

Bede attributes the conversion of the Picts to *St. Minias*, vulgarly called St. Ringau, but this refers to the Southern Picts; who, leaving the errors of idolatry, embraced the true faith by the preaching of this Holy Father, who is said to have been a reverend holy man of the British nation, who had been instructed in the mysteries of religion at Rome, and died in the year 430, twenty years before Palladius. Whether any of the Southern Picts had emigrated to Orkney and Shetland and brought christianity with them, or whether *St. Minias* had been in the Islands before Palladius is uncertain; but this fact is certain, that there is a small Island near the South end of the Mainland, called St. Minian's or Ringau's Island, on which there are the ruins of a church dedicated to this *Saint*.

Wallace and *Brand*, who have written on these Islands, are both of opinion, that Orkney and Shetland formed a part of the ancient kingdom of the Picts. They give an account of two kings, Belus king of Orkney, Holinshead calls him Bladus; and Boethius, Balus; but it is more probably he was called Belus, for there is a stone in the church of Birsa, where probable he had his palace, having Belus engraven on it in very odd ancient characters. The second king of Orkney and Shetland was called Garcus in the time of Caracticus king of the Scots, and it is reported by Boethius, that he and his wife and family were carried captive to Rome by Claudius. Hermarous Shedal, in his general history of the world, speaking of the Emperor Claudius, says, " Quod insulas Orcades adjecit imperio, sexto quo profectus erat mense Romam reditu, and triumphavit maximo apparatu;" (*i. e.*) That he added the Orkney Islands to the Roman Empire, and in six months after he had set out on his expedition returned to Rome, and triumphed with the greatest splendour; but the memory and actions of these kings are buried in silence. From the preceding extracts, it is evident these islands were discovered by the Romans.—That they were considered as the remote part of the Roman Empire. I think we may presume the Romans were several times in these Islands, and that they formed a part of the Pictish nation, and lastly, that Christianity very early flourished in these remote Islands.

It is probable the Picts continued to inhabit and govern these Islands until the time of Kenneth, the second king of the Scots, a warlike prince, who prevailing with his nobles contrary to their inclination (by craft) to engage in a war with the Picts, in which he is said to have routed the Pictish army, and wasted their country with fire and sword, pursuing them even to these Islands: this took place in 854; so that if Shetland was not left without inhabitants only very few remained.

Soon after this* a colony of bold adventurers came over from Norway, concerning whom Torpæus says, " They were all Pagans, and massacred the remaining Christians that were in possession of the Islands, and spared no pains and expence to

* Dr. Edmonston says, " Shetland was colonized from Norway, in the seventh century, but Dr. Hibert, not much before the ninth, which agrees with the date above.

propagate, and establish their Heathenish rites, &c." The cause which led to the colonizing of these Islands from * *Scandinavia* thus accounted for by the Norwegian poets.

Harold Horfagre, (or the fair-haired,) hearing of the transcendent beauty of the princess Gida, and crediting the rumour to its full extent, without even seeing the damsel, commissioned one of his Lords to make her an offer of his hand. *Harold is* not sufficiently renowned, said the ambitious fair one, never will Gida esteem the noble suiter worthy of her love, until he has reduced all Norway under his power.

Harold was not disheartened by these severe conditions, but vowed to neglect his fine golden locks until the subjugation was accomplished.

He was successful: most of the petty princes of Norway yielding to him absolute submission, others, however, less patient of the yoke, sought a voluntary exile in the remote and sterile Islands of Orkney and Shetland.

These valiant Norwegians, whose martial exploits had been so lately sung in their own country, took comfort in their exile when they considered the opportunities of revenge their situation afforded.

Thus did many summers attest the devastation and slaughter with which the coasts of Harold were visited.

The Monarch was at length aroused from his contemptous disregard of these daring hordes, and having collected a fleet immediately put to sea for these Islands, and landed in the Island of Unst, the most northern Island of the group, the place of his landing is still called Haroldswick.

It is very probable that the petty prince or earl, that withstood Harold with such firmness, and made such desperate attacks upon Norway, was *Rolla*, one of the sons of Rognwald, or Guion. After his defeat by Harold, he fled for safety to the Island of *Sodero*, one of the Ferroe Islands, north-west of Shetland; where finding many outlaws and discontented fugi-

---

* Scandinavia is the name given by the ancients to that tract of territory which contains the modern kingdoms of Norway, Sweden, Denmark, Lapland, and Finland.

tives, he addressed their passions, and succeeded in placing himself at their head; and instead of again measuring his sword with his Sovereign, he resorted to his old profession, and endeavoured to make his fortune by plundering the more opulent places of southern Europe. His first attempt was made upon England; but not succeeding, he stood over to the mouth of the Seine, and availed himself of the state to which France was reduced. Rolla, however, did not limit his ambition to the acquisition of booty: he wished permanently to enjoy some of the fine countries he was ravaging; and after many treaties made and broken, he received the Duchy of Normandy from the hands of Charles the Simple, as a fief, together with Gisla, or Gilla, the daughter of the French Monarch in marriage. I make this short digression to shew that one of the first earls of Orkney, became the founder of a family which in a few years gave Sovereigns to England, Naples, and Sicily, and spread the fame of their talents and prowess throughout the world. In order that these Islands and coasts, which Harold had subdued, might no longer be a refuge for his foes, it was necessary that they should be peopled by individuals firm in their allegiance to the Norwegian crown. Harold, therefore, offered Cothness, Orkney, and Shetland, as one earldom to Ronald, Count of Mercia; but this nobleman being more attached to a Norwegian residence, resigned the donation in favour of his brother Siqurd, or Siquardis, who was accordingly the first elected earl of Orkney and Shetland, by king Harold.* He married Beatrix, the daughter of Malcolm III., king of Scotland.

The partition of the vanquished territories among the first colonists would be, in value and extent, regulated by military and civil rank. But in measuring out such allotments, it would be necessary to resort to some familiar standard of valuation.

The Norwegians in the time of Harold, appear to have scarcely known any other than what was suggested by the coarse woollen attire of the country named Wadmall, eight pieces of this description of cloth, each measuring six ells, con-

* See Bell's Geography, vol. i. page 204.

stituted a Merk or Mark, according to this rude standard of comparison. The extent therefore, of each site of land bearing this appellation was originally described by loose stones called Merk stones, or Meishes: there is much uncertainty in its extent; * but generally it may be considered about an acre and a half. They had a coin also which they called a Merk, which was the supposed worth of forty-eight ells of Wadmall, it consisted of somewhat more than an ounce of fine silver.

It appears the land was divided at first into *free land*, which was inclosed, called Odel, or Udal, and the open wilds called *Scattald*, for which a Scat duty was paid. The first proprietors of land were called Udallers, the patch of ground which the possessor had enclosed being exempt from every imposition to which grazing lands were liable: it is possible therefore, that the uncontrolled enjoyment of the soil destined for culture, first suggested the term Odel or Udal, which signifies in the northern language free property or possession.

The *language* and *religion* of the Scandinavians were transplanted with the colony; the gloomy scenery of Shetland was fully in accordance with the character and usages of the religion of the colonists. The majesty and terrors of Odin or Thor, might well be supposed to delight to reside amidst such desolations of nature.

Their religion was a modification of Druidism, which prevailed in Iceland, and the North in general. The sacred books, tenets, rites, &c., with their laws and military prowess, I shall briefly state.

THE RELIGION of the colonists from Norway was a species of Druidism, which was taught in the sacred books of the Scandinavian Pagan religion called the Edda. The Etymology of the word is difficult, some having derived it from Edde in Norse grandmother, thus making it to signify the parent of religion or poetry. Others consider it as reason. There has been also much controversy as to 1st, where it was written? 2nd, and by whom? It is most likely not the composition of one person or one age.

---

* The Shetland merk of land differs in extent of surface, according to the good or inferior quality so as to be rendered uniform in value.

It consists of odes which are thought by some to be the fragments of a much larger work, now lost to the world.

The most important of the poems are the Voluspa or Prophetess, and Vola; a digest of their mythology, short and extremely obscure, and the Havamal, a singular collection of moral precepts professing to be derived from the God Odin. Odin or Woden was their chief divinity. He is supposed to be a great military chief from the east, and is represented as the god of battles, and as killing thousands at a blow.

This palace, which is called Valhalla, was situated in a city named Midgard, where the souls of heroes who fell in battle enjoy supreme felicity.

The future bliss of Valhalla was pictured with a simplicity of description, in which rude luxury and splendour suited the wild and feudal feelings of a barbarous people.

They believed in one universal and beneficent Father by the name of Alfader, but they also acknowledged many other Gods.

They also acknowledged a personified evil principle, under the name of Surter.

They likewise had in their sacred books, "The History of the World," and various fables in the form of the history of *giants*, *dwarfs*, and the human race. Many parts of their sacred writings were very figurative; Hemger is called the knife of Hela, * (Death). A warlike mind is an angry sword; a battle, a storm of blood. The raven is said to rejoice over the hard game of war. A cloud of bloody drops is said to cover the head of the wounded.

The only remains of Pagan temples built by the earliest colonists yet remaining, are in Ust and Fettar, which were used not only as places of worship, but for convocations and justice.

The Druids believed that the peculiar residence of the Deity was among groves of oak, and it was beneath the shade of such trees that Celtic Oratories were constructed; but the

---

* It is from the Scandinavian, Hela, we derive our word Hell, and from Sinna the wife of the evil genus, comes our word Sin.

Scandinavians had no veneration for any trees but the ash. And their temples were frequently built on high places, where trees had not insinuated their roots. The temples in Shetland were nothing but circles of stones; and some, mere furrows scoped out and stones placed loosely in them.

The diameter of the outer circle of that in Unst, is about 67 feet. The one within this is 54 feet, the innermost circle about 40 feet, and a small centre Tumulus of stones, about 11 feet in diameter.

It was customary, on this central heap of stones, to sacrifice human victims to Thor; which was affected by crushing or breaking the spine. These rites were mingled with the duties of legislation. It was at some general convocation for this purpose, after the altars and worshippers of Odin had been sprinkled with the blood of the immolated victim, that the leaders were elected, under a vow, to defend their country, to revenge its injuries, and to extend its boundaries. And it was promised, that if they fell by the sword, they were to be admitted to Valhalla, to the hall of Odin, where they might have the pleasure of daily cutting each other to pieces in battle, but as soon as the hour of repast came, they were to be perfectly restored, and all feast together on boar's flesh, and drink mead out of the skulls of their enemies. They also believed there was a place consisting of nine worlds, where Hela, with the direst horrors, inflicted punishment on all who died of disease or old age.

Nearly related to the Pagan Religion of the Colonists, if not a branch of it, may be considered THEIR SUPERSTITIONS.

They acknowledged four kinds of imaginary beings. The *Trows*, the *Bogues*, the *Fairies*, and the Mermaids. Some elevated Knolls, shrouded in mist and clouds, are, therefore, called Trolhouland, the hill or domicil of Demons or Trows. Several other hills in Shetland are also celebrated for affording within their internal recesses, an habitation for evil genii; the ancient Norwegian term was Trol, now called Trow, which the inhabitants of Ferro call Foddens Kermond, or underground men. In the Edda, they are called Duergar, whose origin is

C

thus stated. Odin and his brothers killed the giant Ymer, from whose wounds ran so much blood, that all the families of the giants were drowned, except one, who saved himself in a bark. These gods then made of those giants bones and of their flesh and blood, the earth, waters and heavens; but in the putrefaction of their bodies, several worms originated, which partook of human shape and reason: these little beings, which were of the most delicate figure, always dwelt in subterraneous caverns or clefts of the rocks: they are said to be remarkable for their activity, riches, and malevolence. It is thought by some, that this has a remote allusion to real history, and that some rays of light are even mingled with this darkness. But whatever may be said to apologize for these fables, persons have been found in every part of the world, who have believed in their existence. But recently the name of fairies has improperly been given to them, which Dr. Hibert supposes of comparatively modern introduction into Europe, being derived from the Persian Peris, an imaginary race of beings, whose offices of benevolence were opposed to the spiteful interference of evil spirits. The Trol, dwelling in the hills of Shetland, are considered as the malevolent beings mentioned in the Edda.

The fairies are described as a people of small stature, gayly dressed in habiliments of green. Brand says, they were frequently seen in Orkney, clad in complete armour; they are said to partake of the nature both of men and spirits, having material bodies, with the means, however, of making themselves invisible. They are said also to have children: they are much addicted to music and dancing; and when they make excursions, it is with imposing effect, being accompanied with most exquisite harmony. The ring made by their tiny feet is considered unholy and hazardous to enter.

> " Like Fairy elves
> Whose midnight revels by a mountain side,
> Or lonely glen, the belated peasant sees,
> Or dreams he sees; while overhead, the moon
> Sits arbitress, and nearest to the earth,
> Wheels her pale course;

> They, on their mirth and dance intent,
> With jocund music charm his ear."

Witches and Warlocks profess to have communion with the "*Guid Folk*," as the Trows are sometimes familiarly called, and have been by them transported in the air from one Island to another, in their visit to Trolhouland and other Knolls of a similar description.

They have been allowed to enter the interior of the hill on one side, and to come out on the other; and in this subterraneous journey they have been dazzled with the splendour exhibited within the recesses through which they have passed: the walls being adorned with gold and silver. The Trows are said to be liable to disease, but they possess among themselves a Catholicon of invaluable efficacy. They are considered dangerous, because they are addicted to the abstraction of the human species, in whose places they leave changelings, the unholy origin of whom, is known by their mental imbecility, or by some wasting disease. Their dreaded visits for these purposes are midnight and noon.

MERMAIDS.—It was their opinion, that beneath the depths of the sea, an atmosphere exists, adapted to the respiring organs of certain beings resembling in form the human race; who are possessed of surpassing beauty, and limited supernatural powers, and liable to death. They dwell in a wide territory of the globe, far below the regions of the fishes, over which the sea, like a cloudy canopy or sky, loftily rolls. They possess habitations constructed of pearly and coralline productions of the ocean. Having lungs adapted to atmospheric air, it would be impossible for them to pass through the volume of waters, that intervenes between the submarine and supra marine worlds, if it were not for the extraordinary power that they inherit, of entering the skin of some animal capable of existing in the sea, which they are enabled to occupy by a kind of demoniacal possession.

One shape they put on is that of an animal, human above the waist; but below, having the body, fins, and tail of a fish. But the most favourable form, is the large seal; for, in possessing an amphibious nature, they are enabled, not only to exist in the ocean, but to land on some rock or island; and leaving the seal vehicle, they resume their proper shape, and, with much curiosity, examine the nature of the upper world. Unfortunately, however, each merman and mermaid possesses but one vehicle or seal skin, enabling the individual to emigrate to their own world again, so that, if they loose it, while visiting the abode of man, the hapless being must perish in the ocean, or become an inhabitant of our earth.

Such were the cunningly devised fables, interwoven with the mythology, of the ancient inhabitants of Orkney and Shetland.

They had also many superstitious notions concerning Lochs and Wells; supposing them to have sanative virtues.

They had a Loch they called Helga water, or the water of health. They also believed in a God that presided over all waters, recognised under the name of Shoopitter, who used to assume, most frequently, the shape of a Shetland pony. This Deity, or water Trow, is the same as is referred to in the Edda, and which recommends prayer to him for success in navigation, fishing, and hunting.

The MILITARY character of the Norwegian colonists would, doubtless, from their former predatory habits, and from their religious notions, be fierce and undaunted. They built a number of Broughs to answer two purposes; to give signal and alarm through the Islands; and, secondly, to retreat to for defence and protection. Their ancient weapons of war were the Stimbarte and Hauberks stein (stone), and barte (an axe) generally made of green porphyry, and hardened and polished so as to be as hard and sharp as iron. The Hauberks were white shields; and the ashen, or spear, the head of which was made of hard porphyry. They also had some headed arrows, many of which kind of weapons have been found of late; several different kinds of which I now have in my possession.

There are many rude pillars standing in various parts of Shetland, supposed to mark the site of some battle, or the grave of some chief.

The laws introduced into the Islands, by the first colonists, it will be interesting briefly to notice. We have seen that temples were used alike for religious and judicial purposes; when for the latter, the central space was devoted to the judge, and the others divided in an order of precedence, for counsellors, men of rank, and the populous. The Judge was called the great Fouda. The counsellors were called Raadmen, which signifies, to see right or justice done.

The place of execution for any criminal condemned by the Fouda, was on the summit of a high hill, named Hanger Hugh, or Heog.

If any accused person, after hearing the sentence of the Fouda, was desirous to appeal to the voice of the people, he was allowed to press, uninjured, from without the precincts of the site that was considered hallowed. A sanctuary was placed at a certain distance, the escape to which depended upon the will of the people. If the popular voice did not accord with the sentence of the Fouda, the accused was allowed to flee to the place of safety, and his life was preserved: but if the popular indignation was against him, he was pursued in his way to the sanctuary, and any one, before he reached it, might put him to death.

A tradition prevails, that whatever criminal ascended the steeps of Hanger Heog, never came down alive: two bodies were found near its base, seventy or eighty years ago. But this system of jurisprudence was not of long continuance. The legislative convocations, and seat of justice, were fixed on a holm in the midst of a fresh water loch, and large stones placed at proper distances through the water to the holm, or else it was near the shore of the sea.

The place was called Thing Valla. It is supposed that king Olaus of Norway, introduced milder laws, which is celebrated in some of their ancient songs, called Vissacks. Tingwall, or Thing Valla, was the residence of the great Fouda, or Lagman, who took an annual circuit round the Islands, distributing justice at the minor lawtings, and was attended in his route by a number of Raadmen as his retinue. From Peterkin's notes, I will give an account of the punishment of several petty, and a few capital crimes, though not of so ancient a date. Some were sentenced to be banished from the Islands, and all their property confiscated, if they were found in the Islands after a month, or the first departure of a vessel. Others were " to be *tane*, and drownit to the death in the example of *utheris :*" and again, " to be *hanget* by the *craige quhill* he die."

I will notice a civil regulation, or two, which will throw some light on the state of the inhabitants, concerning the weights and measures of the Dutch, and other merchants, who come to merchandise with the people, sold by unlawful *Meets*, *Kanns*, *Bismerg*, and weights, whereby they are greatly enriched, and the inhabitants depauperate and hurt thereby, and that they should henceforth sell by the auld custom measures of the country.

Another regulation was, that no vessel, or boat, should transport any one out of the Islands, without a license from the Fouda. And that no land should be sold to any one, until the same be offered to the nearest of the sellers kin, and next to my lord, according to the ancient use and constitution of the country, which makes all such sales null.

I have glanced at the religious superstitions, military prowess, and laws of the Scandinavian colonists, and hasten to inform the reader of the introduction of christianity into the Islands.

Paganism had but a short reign. Christianity was introduced into these Islands, by *Olaus I. king of Norway, in the year 1014, by the point of the sword.

Landing at Ronaldsy, one of the Orknies, he invited earl Siguard, on board one of his vessels, with which request he unsuspectingly complied, and was accompanied by his son Hindus. You are now, said the Monarch, fallen into my power, and I propose to you these conditions, first, to profess with all under your dominion, the Christian Religion, present yourself at the font for baptism, and yield me homage, and consider your possession of the country as due to my courtesy,

* Olas I. called Olans Friquissau. The tutelar Saint of the northern nations, supposed to have been converted to christianity in England. See Bell's Geography, vol. i. page 2 4,

and be my friend for ever; for by obeying the mandates of God, you shall partake his Heavenly Kingdom.

But if, on the other hand, you hesitate to comply with my command, death immediately awaits you. Unless also your people choose to profess upon this very spot what will be their true liberty, the whole of the Islands shall be destroyed by fire and sword. Refuse me, and ye may expect extreme calamity here, and hereafter eternal punishments. The earl replied to the king with much mildness, declaring he could not be induced, by either hope or fear, to prostitute the religion of his Fathers, or deny the established worship of the Gods; for I am not conscious of being more clear sighted than my ancestors; nor do I know, in what respect, that religion, which you command, excels our own.

The king seeing him obstinately bent to idolatry, drew his sword, and seizing upon Hindus, now be assured, said he, I shall keep my word, and I shall spare no one who is opposed to the heavenly God, and to the Gospel. I pray you be not obstinately bent against your own interest, and the interest of those under your dominion, nor against your son; for unless you shall profess yourselves the servants of the Great Deity, whom I revere, your son shall perish before your eyes, and one common destruction shall follow.

The Earl could not resist this powerful argument; he submitted along with his son, and all his people, to baptism; the king left ministers of the Divine word, with other holy men, to give the proselytes further instruction; and taking with him Hindus, as an hostage, he set sail with pious delight, to communicate his success in Norway.

The first Missionary appointed by Olaus, and who baptized the Pagans of Hialtland, was Sigismund Bretteson, a native of Feroe, who is much celebrated for his prowess. But the light of Christianity was, at first, but feeble in its opposition to the dark phantoms of Pagan Mythology. The temples at Unst and Fetlar, dedicated to Odin and Thor, long retained their influence over the popular mind.

Siquard had two sons, named Trophinus and Hindus. The

latter went to Norway, as an hostage; Trophinus built a church at Birsa, on the main land of Orkney, where the first Bishop of Orkney presided. I think it probable Hindus was the eldest son, for Throphinus is said to have defeated Ronald, a grand son of Siquard, who was esteemed the rightful heir, and must have been son to Hindus.

Guthrie also, in his History of Scotland, says, " Malcolm the Third, having no issue to succeed him, except his grandson, by his daughter Beatrix, who was married to a great nobleman, whom Fordun calls the *Ab Thane*, or chief Thane of Dule, which, I suppose to be a corruption of the word Thule. The grandson's name was Duncan, upon whom Malcolm first conferred the principality of Cumberland. In 1084, Duncan mounted the throne of Scotland, as Duncan the 1st. Beatrix, the mother of Duncan, had a daughter also, named Doado, who was married to the Thane of Glamis, who is said to have been mother to the famous Macbeth, who murdered Duncan and succeeded to his throne.

Trophinus left two sons, Paul and Earland, who amicably shared in the government. At this period the Islands are supposed to have reached their acme of improvement and glory.

Their sons, however, did not inherit the dispositions and virtues of their fathers. Magnus, the son of Earland was pious and peaceable, but Hacon or Haequin, the heir of Paul, was vehement, wild, and impatient of restraint: he saw how Magnus was revered, and envy drove him to revenge, and he murdered Magnus. This took place in the beginning of the 12th century. Magnus was the chief christian saint of Orkney and Shetland. He was said to be a meek ruler, worthy of a throne in the Millenium, since he refused to fight against men from whom he had received no injury. He was cruelly put to death by Hacon, with whom he pleaded piously to spare his innocent life; but he was inexorable: he then bent forward his head with true christian fortitude, and the executioner cut it off at a blow. He was sainted by the Pope and a cathedral was afterwards built and dedicated to him at Kirkwall. The present St.

Magnus cathedral members afterwards repaired to his tomb, and, it is said, miracles were performed on such as offered oblations.

Hacquin left two sons, Paul the silent, and Harold the orator. Paul succeeded to the Earldom, but Ronald, a descendant of St. Magnus, an elegant and accomplished youth, appeared at the court of Norway, and was supported in his claims to the earldom as the heir of the canonized saint. He sent messengers to Paul, and offered to share the government with him; but this proposal was rejected. However, by various schemes, Ronald gained his purpose, and shared the government. They lived together amicably until Ronald was, at length, assassinated by a monk, A. D. 1196.

The introduction of Christianity into these Islands, made the people liable to the burdens to which churches are liable, that are subject to the dominion of the Pope.

Orkney and Shetland formed a see, over which a bishop was appointed, who resided in the palace, and officiated in the cathedral at Kirkwall, Orkney. At Tingwall, where the parish church of Scalloway, the capital of Shetland, stood, was the residence of the Archdeacon of the see.

The tithe of wool required for the Pope, was twenty-two cwt. according to the standard of Hialtland, and the cultivated land paid a tenth to the Bishop and Priests.

It appears, from the ruins of catholic places of worship, that the Islands were abundantly supplied with churches and priests.

But, besides the compulsatory contributions, superstition dictated one burden on the lands that was gratuitous. The Bishop introduced and recommended a venerable female as a person of extraordinary sanctity; and that if she slept one night in a parish, the inhabitants would be blessed with plenty of *corn* and *fish;* but the prayers of this matron could scarcely be expected without some pecuniary acknowledgment; accordingly, the inhabitants were induced to allow the holy dame a penny for each merk of land.

Skinner gives an account of Ralph, who was sent by Paul, Earl of the Orcades, to Thurstan, arch-bishop of York, desiring

D

him to be consecrated bishop of these Islands; and this is said to be in conformity to his predecessors; it was accordingly conferred upon him. Guthrie also, in his history of Scotland, says—The archbishop of York, being worn out with age and infirmities, resigned the command of the English army to Ralph, Bishop of the Orkneys, in 1138.

In 1222, we read of Adam, Bishop of Orkney, which included Caithness, whose officers collected his tithes and other dues so rigourously, that the people rose and dragged the Bishop and one of his attendants, Serlo a monk, into his kitchen, and there burnt them both alive. Alexander, king of Scotland, was at Jedburgh, who immediately marched north with an army, and seized 400 of the insurgents, and ordered them all to be gibbetted. The earl of Caithness was strongly suspected of having been privy to the Bishop's murder; but by representing the oppressions the Prelate had been guilty of, and his wanton excommunications, Alexander was content with punishing him with a large fine; but he was shortly after murdered and his house reduced to ashes.

Guthrie gives an account of these Islands being ceded to Norway in 1094, by Donald Bane to Magnus, king of Norway, for the military assistance rendered by the latter to the former. He says the Islands were possibly the appenage of Donald himself, before he usurped the throne; and though this is contrary to the whole of the history and chronology of the Islands, and contradicted by Guthrie himself in another place, both Wallace and Brand, in their histories of Orkney and Shetland, with a little alteration of date, have followed him in this error.

Wallace says, the Norwegians held the Islands 164 years, when they again lost them in 1263, Alexander the Third being then king of Scotland; and gives an account of this conquest of Haco. The only manner that Guthrie and the two latter historians, can be reconciled with this history is, to suppose the Hebrides are confounded with these Islands.

In the 14th century the Earldom was conferred by the king of Denmark to the St. Clairs, or Sinclairs, a Scotch family, but that his heirs male should not succeed to the Earldom without the consent of the king; and if he died without issue, it was to return to the Danish crown, and at Martinmas to pay 1000 nobles of gold English money. The last who was intrusted with it, was Sinclair of Roslin; and, as distant provinces commonly become, in some measure, the property of the governor, we are told that about the year 1379, Sinclair was declared Earl of Orkney, &c., and, after taking the oath of allegiance to Hacquin.

The terms upon which he was to hold his government, have been transmitted to us from an original charter, by the Danish historian Torfæus.

1st. They were to be ready to serve the said king, his heirs and successors, with a hundred good men, well armed, as often as they should be required, upon three months advertisement; providing that the king would maintain them at his own charge, as soon as they should come to his presence.

2nd. To defend the Isles of Orkney and Shetland, in case of their being attacked by any foreign power, not only with the forces that could be raised within these Islands, but also with the whole strength of his other friends and servants, whose assistance he also promised to afford, in case the king of Norway should think fit to attack any foreign state or kingdom.

3rd. Not to impignorate or alienate any part of the said Islands, nor to build castles or fortresses within them, without the express consent of the king.

4th. To protect and maintain the inhabitants thereof, in all their just rights, laws, and liberties.

5th. To be subject to the laws of Norway, and to attend upon the said king when required, either to give him counsel in general assemblies, or to assist him in his wars.

6th. To enter into no private compact or bond with the bishop of Orkney, without the consent of the king, and to assist the king in opposition to the bishop, if need be.

7th. That the said earldom and government should revert into the hands of the said king and his heirs, in case the earl should die without male heirs; and that his children, though heirs male, should not enter upon the succession, without the consent and good will of the said king.

8th. To pay to the said king, in Tunisbury, at the feast of Martinmas next, the sum of 1000 nobles of gold, English money.

And lastly. To prevail with his cousins, Malisius Speire and Alexander de Leard, to give up all their pretensions to the said earldom and Isles.

This agreement was signed by several Scotch Bishops and Knights, as *guarantees* for the performance of the agreement, and that three hostages should remain in Norway.

This transaction is said to be repugnant to the principles of all civil government, as this earl was undoubtedly a native and subject of Scotland; but others say it was with the consent of his own sovereign, the king of Scotland.

It is evident from the above extract, that, though these Islands were, at this time, granted to a Scotch family, the conditions shew they were connected with the crown of Norway. This is much perplexed, by the account given by Wallace, of these Islands being brought into the hands of the family above named, Magnus Speire.

"After the death of Hacquin, Alexander invaded the Isle of Man, and the western Isles, and intended to make the like attempt for the recovery of Orkney and Shetland. Ambassadors were sent to him from Magnus, King of Norway and Denmark, who succeeded, after several treaties.

It was at last agreed, that Alexander should pay to Magnus, the sum of 4000 marks sterling, with the sum of 100 marks a year; and that Magnus should quit all right that he might pretend to the Islands of Orkney and Shetland, and the other Islands of Scotland; which accordingly he did, by letters under his great seal, renouncing and giving over all right and claim that he had, or might have, both for himself and his successors, to these and all the other Isles of Scotland; and for the better confirmation hereof, a marriage was agreed upon, betwixt the lady Margaret, daughter of Alexander, and the son of king Magnus, both children; to be completed when they came to a marriageable estate. Orkney, being in this manner recovered from Norway, it continued, ever after, annexed to the crown of Scotland.

That Alexander gave the Islands to a nobleman surnamed Speire, Earl of Cathness, whose son Magnus Speire, Earl of Caithness and Orkney, &c., was in great repute in the days of king Robert Bruce. But he dying without heirs male, his daughter, Elizabeth Speire, succeeded him in the estate, and was married to Sir William Sinclair.

This account is so confused and incorrect, as I shall shew, that Wallace's history can be considered as no authority; for the very same account is given in Guthric, as the treaty for the *Hebudes* or Hebrides, which are a distinct class of Islands lying in the western ocean.

"The battle of Largs seems to have decided the fate of the little Island, (the Isle of Man,) for I perceive that it submitted, at this time, to Alexander, who undertook to protect it, provided its prince should always have in readiness, ten galleys for the service of the Scots, when required. The submission of Owen, had a great effect on the chiefs of the other Islands belonging to the Norwegians; and Magnus, the son and successor of Hacquin, proposed a treaty with Alexander. Magnus, according to the testimony of all historians, was a wise and learned prince, and very probably thought that his ancestors had been no great gainers, by the troublesome possession of those Hebudæ Islands.

Alexander, at this time, having an army in readiness, instead of listening to any accommodation, sent the Earls of Buchan and Murray, with Allen the chamberlain, and a considerable body of men, to the western Islands; where they put to the sword some of the inhabitants, and hanged their chiefs, for having encouraged the Norwegian invasion. Magnus, who had by this time returned to Norway, sent the Bishop of Hamer (so called by Fordun), and his chancellor, as his ambassadors to Alexander, offering him restitution of the Isles of Bute and Arran, provided he was left in quiet possession of the Hebudæ. Alexander rejected this proposal with indignation; and the Bishop returning home, represented to Magnus the danger he was in of losing the whole; upon which, a fresh embassy was sent to Scotland, consisting of Norwegian noblemen, with their chancellor at their head. After some conferences a treaty was concluded, by which Magnus renounced all right in those Islands, which either his father, or any of his predecessors, claimed or possessed; but Alexander undertook to pay one thousand marks of silver, in two years, to Magnus,* and one hundred marks yearly for ever. This annual to Norway, was thought by many of the Scots disgraceful, and the payment being suspended, *ceased* after much litigation; for if the cession made by Donald Bane, was with a reservation of superiority to the kings of Scotland, the paying an annual tribute for restoring them, was not very consistant with Alexander's dignity. It concludes with an account of the marriage contract mentioned by Wallace. It is evident from this extract, that Wallace has confounded some facts concerning Orkney and Shetland, with the history of another groupe of Islands, and this error has been frequently copied. Though Orkney and Shetland were conferred upon a Scotch family, 1 think I have shewn they were not ceded to Scotland, but continued a part of the kingdom of Norway.

We are told by Torfæus, that when Erie of Pomerania, was recognised as the lawful heir of the kingdom of Norway, Henry Sinclair, as the first temporal peer of the kingdom, signed the recognition.

Three years after this, the earl killed Malisius Speire and seven others, through which he probably lost his earldom. "The lordly line of high St. Clair," assumed the title of princes of Orkney.

In 1418, the earldom was divided into two; Orkney was given to Thomas de Tholach, or Tullock, the bishop; and Shetland to John Sinclair. The bishop soon resigned it to David Menzies of Weem. In 1434, the Sinclairs were restored to the earldom, but not before he had agreed to accept it on the terms on which his grand-father, Henry, had it before him, and to demolish a fortress, which that nobleman had built without the consent of the king of Denmark.

* Hearne's Edition of Fordun says, " Four Thousand," which is followed by Buchanan.

The kings of Norway had always kept the full and entire possession of these northern Islands, to the great mortification of the Scots, as they had a full persuasion that they formed part of the Pictish dominions, to which they had succeeded. Upon the accession of Christiern the First, to the crowns of Denmark and Norway, the arrears of the annual, for the ceding of the Hebrides, amounted to 43,000 marks, including penalties for the non-payment of which. This, Christiern demanded with some roughness from James the Second; both parties agreed to refer their differences to Charles, king of France. A congress was therefore appointed in 1457, to be composed of ministers of the two crowns. But the congress was not held until 1460, and the French king dismissed the case, and proposed to terminate all differences between the crowns of Scotland and Denmark, by a marriage of Margaret, Christiern's daughter, with the Prince Royal of Scotland—upon the terms of

I.—The entire abolition of the annual of Norway.

II.—The Uniting of Orkney and Shetland to the crown of Scotland, for ever.

III.—That Christiern should advance with his daughter, a hundred thousand crowns in ready money, that she might be in condition to appear in splendour equal to her quality.

The Danish ambassadors said, they had no instructions on that head, but would acquaint the king with the proposals.

On account of the great difficulties attending the perpetual cession of these Isles to the crown of Scotland, Christiern finally agreed to the marriage, on the following terms:—

I.—That the annual of Norway should be remitted, and for ever extinguished.

II.—That king Christiern should give 60,000 florins of gold for his daughter's portion; whereof 10,000 should be paid before her departure from Denmark; and that the Islands of Orkney should be made over to Scotland, by way of pledge for the security of the remainder; with this express proviso, that they should return to Norway after the payment of the sum.

From this contract it appears, that, in fact, the Orkney Islands were only mortgaged for the remainder of the brides fortune, and that the Scots had greatly abated of the demands they had made at the Court of France. It happened, however, at the time when the articles came to be executed, that Christiern was engaged in an unsuccessful war with the revolting Swedes and other enemies, and found himself unable to advance the 10,000 florins which he had engaged to pay down at his daughter's departure. He was, therefore, obliged to apply to the plenipotentiaries to accept of 2000, and to take a further mortgage of the Shetland Isles for the other 8000; in which request he was gratified, and the negotiation was finished the 10th of May, 1469. In the Scottish Historical Library, Lib. 8, p. 30-3,) adds, "upon queen Margaret's being brought to bed of a young prince, king Christiern of Denmark made an absolute deed, and for ever quitted his claim to these dominions."

The first grant of them by the king of Scotland, was to William Tulloch, the bishop of Orkney; the crown rent being £120, with 5 chalders of Bear, and 120 salt marts; making in the whole, £466. 13s. 4d. Scots; his lease, or tack, was renewed for three years.

From this to 1530, the Civil Government was committed to *lieutenants* and *viceroys*, and the *ecclesiastical* jurisdiction was assigned to the archbishop of St. Andrews.

In 1530, king James the Fifth was induced to make an hereditary grant of the estate of the crown in Orkney and Shetland, to his natural brother James, earl of Moray. The islanders, seeing that a feudal superior was intended to be interposed between them and the Sovereign, they were afraid the ancient laws of the country were about to suffer a correspondent change. Headed by Sir James Sinclair, the governor of Orkney, they arose in arms to resist this arbitrary innovation. The earl of Caithness, the earl of Moray's kinsman, was sent out against them. The *Udallers* met their opponents on the confines of Stennis, and in a sanguinary engagement, the earl of Caithness was defeated, and about 5000 of his followers were slain, and the rest taken prisoners.

When the king heard the result of the engagement, so far

from taking vengeance on the Udallers, he appeared in his sub-sequent conduct, sensible of the justice of their cause; and that the intended dominion of a Mesne lord was an attempt to trans-fer them from the hands of the king of Scotland, to whose immediate protection they had been committed by their former king.

The promoters, therefore, of the insurrection were pardoned, and the Governor of Orkney, not only restored, but received various gifts from the royal favour; so that the Islands conti-nued connected with the crown till the reign of Queen Mary.

In 1565, Queen Mary made an hereditary grant of the crown's patrimony in these Islands, and of superiority over the free tenants, to her natural brother, Lord Robert Stewart, the abbot of Holyrood house, in consideration of an annual payment.

At this time the reformation was introduced into Scotland; and an act of parliament had passed, declaring that the third of all popish benefices should be set apart for the support of paro-chial ministers. Lord Robert was intrusted with this control over the churches and Bishoprick, which was not cordially approved.

In 1567, Earl Bothwell was created Duke of Orkney, by Queen Mary, and was said to be a dignity conferred upon him to make him the more worthy to be her husband. This took place through some exchange between Lord Robert and Earl Bothwell. He was married to the Queen of Scotland, by Adam Bothwell, Bishop of Orkney, in the palace of Holyrood house, after the manner of the reformed church, on the 27th of May, 1567. He being much disliked by the nobility for his marriage with the Queen, and for a suspicion they had that he was the murderer of her former husband, for a place of security and retreat, he built the Castle of Noutland, in Westra, one of the Orkneys, to retreat to in case of a storm. And soon it came to pass: for being deserted by the Queen at Carberry hill, and persuaded by the lords of the congregation, he made to sea with two or three ships, which he had prepared before hand, for that purpose.

He fled to Orkney, but being refused admittance to Kirkwall

E

Castle, and his Castle in Westra not being fully finished, he betooke himself again to sea, and made for Shetland. He was closely pursued by William Kirkaldie of Grange, in the *Unicorn.* Kirkaldie entering the south end of Brassay sound, came in sight of him as he was leaving the North mouth of the harbour; and following Bothwell's track, who ordered the pilot to pass close to a blind rock, on which Kirkaldie's ship, the Unicorn, struck, and was wrecked. This rock is now called the Unicorn from this circumstance. Bothwell made over for Norway, where, it is said, he was apprehended and imprisoned.

In 1581, the Islands reverted to Lord Robert Stewart, who built or repaired the palace of Birsa, the chief residence of the Earls of Orkney, placing this inscription above the gate; " Dominus Robertus Stewartus Filius Jacobi quinti *Regis* Scotorum hoc opus instruxit"—which inscription, together with the motto, (" sic fuit, est et erit.")—he took above his *coat* of arms; and which in after time injured his son.

He also built a seat on the main land of Shetland, near Sumburgh head, the ruins of which are yet standing, and which are called the Lords houses.

The reformed religion being introduced by so unworthy a professor of it as the cidevant abbot of Holyrood house, no wonder that it should be necessary, at a very late period, to issue out acts at Kirkwall, forbidding, under severe penalties, all idolatry, pilgrimages, &c. So many relicks of popery remained, that it led the reformed clergy to complain, that the people preferred the old catholic places to the new; they therefore recommended them to be razed to the ground.

Episcopacy was established before the close of the sixteenth century; for King James VI, when only one year old, was anointed, and then crowned, by Adam Bothwell, Bishop of Orkney and Shetland, in the parish kirk of Sterling, in July, 1567, according to the reformed religion. Robert Steward, the Earl of Orkney, obtained after this, the bishoprick from bishop Bothwell, in exchange for the abbacy of Holyrood house; so that he became sole Lord of the whole country, and he and his son Patrick, who succeeded him, did in the church what they pleased.

After fifty years of confusion, episcopacy was again restored; and, in 1610, James Law was made Bishop; and the Earldom was united to the crown, by the death and forfeiture of Patrick Steward. The account of whom I cannot better give, than by an extract from Pitcarn's criminal trials :—

" Patrick Steward was the son to Robert Steward, who was an illegitimate son of James the Fifth.

He exercised Royal power within the distant Isles of Orkney and Shetland, where his mandates had the force of laws, against which the voice of the oppressed Islanders was far too weak, to make itself heard. This haughty savage exacted from his subjects, engagements in which they became bound to support his quarrel against every man, without the exception of the king himself.

The subscribers of these treasonable obligations, moreover, bound themselves to be judged by the said Earl, without reserving or acknowledging any appeal to king, councel, or session; a thing, says the indictment, " unnatural, unjust, and tyrannical, impossible, and treasonable."

He was also accused of interrupting the passages and ferries of Orkney and Shetland, so that none should be allowed to use them without his own special license; and those who transgressed this petty tyrants mandate, were subject to ruinous fines and imprisonments. Nor was the property of the king's tenants in these Islands more secure than their personal liberty.

The earl altered at his own pleasure, and always to his own advantage, the acknowledged standards of coins, weights, and measures, current through the Islands. In erecting his castle of Scalloway, and other expensive edifices, the kings tenants were forced to work in quarries, transport stone and lime, dig, delve, climb, and build, and submit to all possible sorts of servile and painful labour, without either meat, drink, hire, or recompense of any kind; finally, says the indictment, the said earl has treasonably discharged the said inhabitants of Orkney and Shetland, to buy or sell meal, malt, meat, drink, fish, flesh, butter, cattle, sheep, or other commodity, without his license, under severe penalties; which severe penalties were levied by imprisonment, or forfeiture, and sometimes capitally, at the pleasure of the earl.

He was apprehended in Shetland, where he had concealed himself in a secret chamber, made in the wall of the ruins of his father's house, at Sumburgh; he was conveyed to Edinburgh castle, and from thence to Dunbarton castle. His extravagances had obliged him to mortgage his estate to Sir John Arnot; and James the Sixth, by purchasing the mortgage, ordered the Sheriff to take possession of the earldom, and its castles. The earl, though a prisoner, stormed at this proceeding, and gave a commission to his illegitimate son, Robert Steward, to retake the castles; which he accordingly did, and stood in open rebellion against the royal authority. A commission for reducing him was sent down to the earl of Caithness, who besieged and took the castle of Kirkwall, and sent Robert Steward and his accomplices, prisoners to Edinburgh.

Patrick Steward, the noted oppressor, was tried for treason and rebellion; he was condemned, and beheaded at the cross in Edinburgh, in Feb. 1615. His son and chief accomplices were tried at the same place, and hanged as traitors.

After the death of Patrick Steward, the temporalities of the bishoprick were restored. These had been frequent quarrels and mischiefs between the former earls and bishops, and their vassals, because their lands lay intermixed. But now, James the Sixth separated the earldom and bishoprick, and the bishop was made sole judge within his own bounds. Bishop Law was much respected, and often employed in important matters by the king; and was at length translated to the archbishoprick of Glasgow.

To him succeeded George Graham, who was translated from the see of Dumblane. He continued in the bishoprick twenty-three years. But when the contention raged about prelacy and the liturgy, he abjured episcopacy, and submitted to the covenanters; and in the year 1638, at the assembly in Glasgow, he resigned his bishoprick.

King Charles the First, after Graham had been divested of the bishoprick, promoted Dr. Robert Barron, professor of

Divinity in the Marischal College of Aberdeen, to the bishop-rick; but being forced to fly to Berwick, he there died before his consecration.

In 1662, episcopacy being restored by Charles the Second, four more bishops, for a short time, were permitted to retain the see. The first, Thomas St. Serf; the second, Andrew Honyman; the third, Murdock Mackenzie; and in 1688, Andrew Bruce, who was the last bishop of these Islands;* many of whom were extraordinary in learning or benevolence, and in being employed in important matters of state.

It appears, however, that many of the non-conforming ministers in Shetland, held their livings during this latter prevalency of episcopacy; which is accounted for on the ground of their remote situation. Not only did Patrick Steward's death restore the temporalities of the bishoprick, but the whole Islands came into the full possession of the king; and a proclamation to all his majesty's liege subjects, that they were perpetually and inseparably annexed to the crown. Sir James Stuart, Lord Ocheltree, was made the Sheriff of them. After him, others succeeded to be governors, until the year 1647, at which time William Douglass, Earl of Morton, got a wadset, or mortgage, of the Islands, from Charles the First.

To him succeeded his son Robert Douglass, Earl of Morton, in 1649; in which year the Marquis of Montrose came from Holland to these Islands, and stayed a few months in Kirkwall, and there raised some forces, most of which were either killed or taken prisoners at the unfortunate encounter of Cabersdale.

---

* The last episcopal clergyman in these Islands, was the Reverend —— Hunter, whose unwearied assiduity in discharging the duties of his office, attended with great fatigue of body, and often at the imminent risk of his life, on these boisterous seas, endeared him to the people under his pastoral care, and made his memory precious among them. The Rev. John Skinner, father of Bishop Skinner, married Mr. Hunter's eldest daughter, when he was the tutor to the only son of Mr. Sinclair, Laird of Scolloway. Mr. Hunter had an episcopal church at Lunna, but he travelled over the Islands, and performed service in the houses of several of the best families. With him died episcopacy in Shetland. The Presbyterians called him 'pack Billy,' as he carried a change of raiment with him.

To him, succeeded to the possession of the Islands, his son William Douglass, Earl of Morton, in 1664. In the first Dutch wars, there was a ship called the Carmelan, of Amsterdam, which was wrecked on the Skerries, near the mainland of Shetland, in which, it is said, there were many chests of coined gold, that were seized on by some who professed to act for the Earl. Whereupon, the Lords of the treasury called the Earl to an account, and so redeemed the mortgage of the Islands, and obtained a decreet of declaration against him.

And December 17th, 1669, an act was passed for the annexation of Orkney and Shetland to the crown of Scotland, and erected into a stewarty.

As I have the Act of Parliament in my possession I will here transcribe it.

" Forasmuch, as the Isles of Orkney and Shetland are a great, and so considerable a part of his majesty's ancient kingdom, that for divers ages they were the occasion of much trouble and expence of blood and money, for maintaining against the invasion of foreigners, and recovering the same out of their hands by armies and treaties, and the said Isles being of a great and large extent of bounds, and so remote and at such a distance from the ordinary seat of justice and judicatories, that the inhabitants within the same, are not able to travel in the winter season, and at other times cannot, without great trouble and expence, repair to the said judicatories, to complain where they are oppressed and grieved: it is not only fit, in order to his majesty's interest, but will be to the great advantage of his majesty's subjects, dwelling there, that, without interposing any other lord or superior betwixt his majesty and them, they should have an immediate dependance upon his majesty and his officers, being their great security against foreign attempts and oppressions.

And seeing it is most expedient and necessary for the public revenue, and as diverse annexations have been made, from time to time, of the Earldom of Orkney, and Lordship of Shetland, with the pertinants of the same.

These took place in 1540 and in 1612. And yet, importunity prevailing with his majesty, and his royal father, their goodness and inclination to gratify their subjects, they were induced to give them away, and part with so great a jewel of their crown, and to dispose and grant rights of the said earldom and lordship, which being found to be to the great prejudice of his majesty's crown and subjects, and contrary to the laws and acts of parliament of Scotland. (From the laws and acts made in the first parliament of Charles the Second, p. 121.

And further, his majesty doth of new again unite, annex, and incorporate to his crown of this his ancient kingdom, to remain inseparably with the same, in all time coming, the said earldom and lordship, with all and sundry Isles, holms, udal lands, and all other lands whatever, of what name, and by what designation soever, the same are or may be known, lying within the sheriffdom of Orkney, and pertaining to the said earldom and lordship, and belonging to his majesty, in manner foresaid, in property or superiority, or by any other right or title, together with all castles, towers, fortalices, milns, multers, fishings, annual rents, reversions, patronages of kirks and tiends, parsonage and vicarage pertaining to his majesty, within the bounds foresaid; and all and whatsoever mines of gold, silver, copper, and other minerals, within the foresaid bounds; with the heritable office of justiciary, sheriffship, and foudrie, and admirality, with all other parts, pendickles, and pertinants, casualties, privileges, and jurisdictions, offices, and others whatsoever pertaining to the same—all which, his majesty with consent foresaid, doth unite and annex to the crown. And further, his majesty with advice and consent of the estates foresaid, hath suppressed the said office of sheriffship, and hath erected, and hereby erects a stewarty within the bounds foresaid, to be called in all time coming the stewarty of Orkney and Shetland. Ordaining the tenants, possessors, and inhabitants, within the bounds foresaid, and other persons who were formerly answerable and liable to the jurisdiction of Sheriffship and Foudrie above mentioned, to be answerable to his majesty's stewart of the said stewarty, and that the said office of stewarty shall not be given heritably to any person or persons, and their heirs, without advice and consent of the parliament." This annexation was not to prejudice the bishop of Orkney of his patrimony and privileges, &c, nor to the prejudice of his majesty's vassals, within the said Isles, of their liberty and privilege, to have, and send commissioners to parliament, to represent them in the same manner as they did, or might have done, formerly, &c.

The king's exchequer gave a lease of the stewarty, at a sale, to the highest bidder. In Wallace's time, it was let as low as eighteen hundred pounds, although, in the earl of Morton's time, it was reckoned to be worth three thousand five hundred. The lease was for three or five years, and then again relet.

The government of the steward was in the king's bound; the manner and precedure of his jurisdiction is after the form of sheriffship, the title only differing.

In 1707, the grant in favour of the earl of Morton, did not convey to him the superiority of any lands held by vassals under investitures from the crown, prior to the grant to Robert Stewart, and who had not taken renewals.

In 1778, in a memorial concerning the teinds, it is said, the tack of the Islands was granted, by the crown, to Mr. Dundas of Castlecary, which included the teinds of the crown. Sir L. Dundas was in possession of the Islands in 1788, and appealed to the judgment of the House of Lords, against the heritors, to determine a point of right to some casualties which were not rightly ascertained. At present the droits of admirality and the crown lands, with the patronage of the churches, belong to Lord Dundas. The principal land owners now are called Lairds, who are descendants of gentlemen who came over from Scotland and purchased landed property from the Udallers.

In 1781, the land holders drew up a memorial, for the purpose of taking legal advice, to remove their political disfranchisement, by being admitted to vote for a representative in parliament. But though their efforts were strenuous and continued for many years, they were without success.

In 1824 or 1825, however, the privilege was granted, but never enjoyed until the reformed act took place. They now send from Orkney and Shetland a member for the county;

and Mr. Balfour of *Kirkwall* and Shapinsha, was the member in 1836. The whole of the Islands now form the most northern county in the kingdom, and have a sheriff in Orkney, and an under sheriff in Shetland. The only court in Shetland is in Lerwick, which consists of Mr. Duncan the under sheriff; two bailies, Mr. C. Ogilvey, and Mr. Spence; the Procurator Fischal Mr. Greig; and several of the Lairds who are magistrates.

They only try petty offences; capital crimes are sent over to Edinburgh, although, I believe such has not been the case for this last century; which must arise, either from the absence of capital crime, or negligence in bringing them to justice for fear of the expense.

It appears that in 1611, there was an act passed, in the castle of Scalloway, for the better and more uniform administration of law, part of which runs thus: "Notwithstanding it is of verity that some persons bearing power of magistracy within the bounds of Orkney and Shetland, have, thir divers yeirs by gane, maist unlauchfully tane upon them, for their own private gain and commodity, to judge the inhabitants of the same countries by foreyne lawis, and sometimes by the proper lawis of this kingdom, as thai found matter of private gain and commodity, in high contempt of our sovereign Lord, and to the great hurt and prejudice of his majesty's subjects. Therefore, the lords of secret counsel have discharged, and by tenor hereof discharge, the said foreign lawis, ordaining the same to be no further usit within the said county of Orkney and Shetland," so that the laws are now much more correctly administered than formerly; but their are still by laws, called country acts, in force; and the patriarchal character of the Lairds enables them to settle many litigations and immoralities, according to the country acts, or at the kirk sessions.

There is in every parish a *Rancelman* who is a sort of half judicial and half ecclesiastical officer, uniting the offices of constable and overseer, pinder and inspector general. I will here insert the 26th act from the country acts *anent* making of Rancelmen and their instructions.

In a Ballie court lawfully *fenced*, the whole householders

F

being present, the Ballie is to cause his clerk read out of such honest men in the parish, being present, as are fit to be Rancelmen; and then he is to inquire of each of them if they are willing to accept of the office of Rancelman; and if any of them refuse, and can give no good reason for his refusal, the Ballie may fine him in ten pound scots and more. They that accept, the Ballie is to inquire of the householders present, if they have ought to object against either of these men, why they should not be made Rancelmen; and, no objection being made, then the following instructions are to be read to them.

I.—You are, at any time of night or day you see needful for, to call for assistance and to enter into any house within the parish, and search the same as narrowly as you can; and upon any suspicion of theft, if they refuse you keys, you are to break open their doors or chests; and if you find anything that is stolen, you are to bring the *fang* and thief to the Ballie or Sheriff. If you have any scruple about anything you find in the house, you are to inquire how they came by it; and, if they refuse it, still you are to take witnesses upon their refusal, and let the thing be secured, until you acquaint the Ballie; you are also to examine the house, stores of flesh and meal, and see if that be correspondent with stock; and likewise, the wool stockings, yarn webs, &c., and inquire how they came by all these; and if they cannot give a satisfactory account thereof, you are to inform against them.

II.—You are to inquire into the conversations of the families; whether there is any discord or unbecoming carriage betwixt husband and wife, *parents* and *children*, master and servant; or any other unchristian or unlawful practice in the family. You are to rebuke such and exhort them to amend; if they obey it, well: if not, you are faithfully to represent such to the judicatory competent, and bring the best evidence you can against all such offenders.

III.—You are to prevent all quarrels and scolding, as far as in you power, by commanding the contending parties to peace; and, if they persist, require witnesses against them, and call for assistance to separate them; and give in a faithful report thereof to the fischal, or clerk of the court; and in case you are not witness to any scolding or quarrelling that happens, you are to gather the best information thereof you can, and make report of the same as aforesaid.

IV.—If you hear any person cursing or swearing, you are to demand of them the fine; and, if they refuse to pay it, you are to require witness against them, and report it to the court: one third is to yourself, and two thirds to the poor.

V.—That you narrowly inquire into your neighbourhood, who sits at home from the kirk on the Sabbath day, and from diets, and catechising; and, if they can give no sufficient reason for their so doing, that you cause them to pay the fine, to be applied as aforesaid; and that you take particular notice in your neighbourhood, anent keeping the Sabbath day: and, if you find any breach thereof, that you report the same.

VI.—You are strictly to observe the country acts, anent keeping good neighbourhood; such as, that none injure others in the grass and corn; and rebuke the offenders with certificates if any continue so to do, you will inform the court against them; and that they build their dycks sufficiently and timously, under the pain contained in the act.

VII.—That tenants do not abuse their land, nor demolish their houses, through sloth or carelessness; that you reprove such, and if they continue so to do, acquaint the land master.

VIII.—You are to inquire if there is any in your neighbourhood, any idle, vagabond persons, and to acquaint such that they must either take some employment to themselves, or you will inform against them, so as they may be punished, and ordered to service; and further, that the poor be taken care of in their respective quarters, and not suffered to stray abroad; nor are you to allow any beggar or thiggar from any other parish to pass through your bounds; and if they offer so to do you will secure them till they be punished conform to the country acts.

IX.—That you try all the dogs in your quarter, and that none be allowed to keep a dog that can take a sheep, unless he be allowed by the Ballie; and that none keep scar dogs, otherwise than in the act allowed; and that the acts be observed anent pending, marking, and taking of sheep.

X.—You are to inquire in your quarter, anent any persons using any manner of witchery, charms, or any abominable and develish superstitions; and faithfully inform against such, so as they may be brought to condign punishment.

XI.—You are to examine all tradesmen in your bounds, and see that they make sufficient work, and do not impose upon any in their prices; and, if you find any such transgressors, that you inform against them, so as they may be punished as the law directs.

XII.—Upon any suspicion of theft, two or three rancelmen may take as many witnesses with them, and go to the neighbouring parish and Rancel; and, if you catch a thief, you are to acquaint the Ballie of that parish thereof, who will order the thief to be secured. And, in the last place, as you are intrusted with the power of inspecting the lives and manners of others, so let your own life and conversation be exemplary unto them for good; and take care you are not found guilty of the faults you are called to reprove in others; for if you should, your punishment shall be double to theirs. They are then sworn, as far as in their power, to attend to all these things.

The country acts are principally resorted to, for the purpose of settling petty litigations which are constantly occurring on account of the uninclosed state of the land; and their riggs being intermixed; and cattle straying and doing damage; and many other causes of discord, to the great injury of vital religion and good neighbourhood. But in other legal transactions the Islands are subject to the laws of Scotland.

The political importance of the Islands to England, is far from being inconsiderable, in point of territory or extent.

The Orkneys and Shetland are equal to the county of Huntingdon, or the principality of Neufchatel in Switzerland; and not at all inferior, in this respect, to Zealand, which is the third of the united provinces.

Secondly, considering their situation, it would be disadvantageous if they did not belong to us. Their advantage is great in a maritime point of view: it is of advantage to have so many good harbours in these rough seas, to put into as occasion may serve; it is important to the whale ships which call and take in many supplies, and half their number of men, at a cheap rate. They also supply our navy with thousands of first rate seamen.

Thirdly, they are important as fishing stations, to supply our markets with dried salt fish, herrings, &c. The exports from Shetland, are fish, oil, kelp, butter, beef, hides, skins, tallow, stockings, and gloves.

The imports consist of ropes, hooks, iron, wood, and most of the necessaries and luxuries of life; drapery, grocery, ale, wine, spirits, &c. Dr. Edmonston states the exports at thirty or forty thousand pounds annually. But I should think, now, on account of the improved state of the herring fishing, the exports are nearly double that sum. The imports, he states at forty or fifty thousand pounds annually; which also, of late, is greatly augmented. To make up the difference between the exports and imports, he notices the pensioners and officers under government; the money brought into the Islands by the whalers, and other vessels; so that there is a supposed balance of twelve or fourteen thousand pounds brought into the Islands annually.

PART THE SECOND.

A DESCRIPTION OF THE ISLANDS.

THESE Islands were but imperfectly known by the ancients, in whose charts they were diversely placed, and variously described. Their ancient name was Ultima Thule, which signifies the end or tail of the world. But the Norwegians called them Hethland, Hiatland, and Schetland; but now they are generally termed Zetland, or the Shetland Islands, and this is supposed to be derived from Yet Land, Hether land, or High land. They are situated in the North Seas, from a little under 60 to 61° 9' N. latitude, and Longitude 1° 6' W. of Greenwich. The nearest continent to the principal Island is Norway; the Port of Bergen being 44 leagues East; whereas they are 46 leagues N.N.E. from Buchanness, the North of Scotland. But the port to which the Islanders generally trade is *Leith*, which is distant about 350 miles.

The number of these Islands has been variously stated; some have said eighty, others one hundred; but many of them are but small holms and some uninhabited islets; others have but one or two families upon them. So that there are but about fifteen of much importance.

The number of inhabitants in the whole of the Islands, is from twenty-six to thirty thousand. The principal Island is called the *Mainland;* which is very much larger than any of the rest. The other Islands are scattered all round it. *The Fair Isle* lies about twenty-five miles South and by West of the Mainland.

Foula lies about twenty miles West of the middle of the Mainland; the small Islands of Havery, Burra, Tronsay,

Papa Stour, and Muckle Rooe, are all on the West of the Mainland, and within a short distance.

Unst is the most Northern Island, which is separated from the North end of the Mainland, by a rapid sound half a mile across, called Blomel Sound.

Yell, Fetlar, Whalsey, and the Skerries, are from seven to twenty miles distant from the Mainland East; and Brossa, Noss, and Mousa, are more South, but they are also East of the Mainland, and from it but a short distance.

But, before I give a particular account of each Island, I shall give a general description of the appearance of the whole of them, and a few particulars as to the climate.

The aspect is bleak and wild; the hills having a dark, sterile, naked appearance, being thinly clad with stunted heather; and frequently the bare rocks appearing above the surface, without any kind of foliage to relieve the eye in its wanderings over these dreary scenes.

The coast is very rocky, and often presents a very shattered and rugged appearance; and frequently rises into lofty and commanding promontories, which stand firm against the violence and encroachments of the deep; and frequently, when the mighty surges break upon them, the contrast is very striking between the whiteness of the surf and the blackness of the rocks.

The Mainland is so intersected by arms of the sea, called voes, and by bays and large fresh water lochs; and having so many Islands scattered around it, at no considerable distance, that it has been considered as the skeleton of a country, or a land escaped from some great disruption.

The hills are generally round backed, a kind of half circle; great numbers of them are thrown confusedly together; the few of them approaching to the conical, are generally more lofty and detached. The east side of the Mainland, and indeed of all the larger Islands, is comparatively low; but on the west, it is lofty and precipitous.

But though the general appearance is by no means attractive, when more closely examined there are many parts, near the coast, tolerably well cultivated. Some of the valleys are equal to many parts of Scotland, but having no regular roads or extensive enclosures, it has a bleak appearance. But whilst the spots of cultivation are few, the romantic and wild simplicity of nature is abundantly displayed; and from the top of some of the lofty hills, the sea views are very sublime, as the ocean may be seen nearly all round, stretching to the horizon. Miss Campbell, a Shetland poetess, has given a beautiful, but rather too highly coloured description, with which I will close this general description.

> " In Nature's wildest robe arrayed,
> Beneath an ever clouded sky ;
> Where round each coast, with hollow roar,
> The rude winds keep their viewless court ;
> Where ceaseless billows dash the shore,
> And Spirits of the storm resort."

THE CLIMATE.—It would naturally be supposed, that on account of the northern situation of the Islands, the cold would be very intense; but it is not so, for there is less frost and snow here than in England, and the hail and snow lie but a short time, on account of the contiguity of every part to the sea. But in the winter, the rain is frequent and heavy, which leaves a humidness in the atmosphere. Dreadful storms prevail, particularly from the west and south west, and we have frequently strong gales from other quarters; so that shipwrecks are not uncommon on these rocky shores. There is very little thunder and lightning, and what there is accompanies the winter storms. The summer of 1834 was exceedingly fine, and differed but little from a summer in England; but the sun was not quite so powerful, nor the weather so steady. Nothing can excel the stillness, serenity, and beauty, of a summer's evening in Shetland :—for from the latter end of May, to the beginning of August, there is no darkness; for the short time the sun sinks below the horizon, his absence is supplied by a bright twilight. But in winter the days are exceedingly short and dull. The latter end of December, the sun rises at half-past nine, and sets forty-two minutes past two. The aurora-borealis is frequent and beautiful during this season. I have seen them shoot from every quarter of the heavens at the same instant, and rush in one light-flame to the centre of the sky, changing every moment their hues and shapes, and affording light and entertainment during the long winter nights.

Upon the whole, I do not consider the climate unhealthy; for the saline particles counteract its humidity. Many of the inhabitants are subject to severe colds and coughs. Scorbutic and chronic diseases, and stomach complaints, are frequent; but these arise, more from their labour and diet, than from the climate. The inhabitants live to a good old oge, and there are some instances of peculiar longevity.

We may say the summer is not so hot, nor the winter so cold, as in England. The medium of temperature is said, by Dr. Edmonstone, to be in Winter 35°; and in Summer, by Farenheit's thermometer, it was a few days 75° in the shade, and to 70°; it is seldom, in winter, more than 10° below the freezing poinf of Farenheit. The medium is said again to be generally 38° in winter; 65° in summer.

This is surprising, in a north latitude nearly reaching to 62°; but it is said the saline particles emit caloric, which being left in the air, makes the atmosphere warmer; and that the wind, in passing over thousands of miles of sea, looses its keenness.

I shall now give a particular account of each Island in the order before named.

THE FAIR ISLE.—The Fair Isle is situated between the most northern of the Orkney Islands, and the south end of the *Mainland* of Shetland. It belongs to an Orkney Laird, Mr. Stewart of Westra, but it pays tiends to, and forms part of, the parish of Dunrossness.

The name is supposed to be a corruption of the Norse word Fioer, that is, distant; or Faar,* which signifies a sheep, as there is belonging to this Island a holm of a curious shape, called the sheep craig.

* There are a groupe of Danish Islands about 100 miles N.W. of Shetland, called North Feroe; which supposes an Island south of that name.

G

The Island is a lofty, precipitous rock, rising where two sets meet, the North sea and the Atlantic ocean; and is surrounded by what is termed a Roost, which consists of rough and troubled seas, arising from contrary currents conflicting, forming whirls and welchies, and frequently running at a rapid rate, in contrary directions, within a few hundred yards, which makes the Island difficult of access, and, frequently, for months it is quite inaccessible.

The Island is about three miles square, and contains about 100 merks of rental land, and about 280 inhabitants. Formerly it had more; but the present number is too many for the size of the Island and the land cultivated. The situation exposes the crops, in winter, to the spray of the sea, which frequently, in rough winters, destroys the seed in the ground; and also to blighting sea breezes in spring; so that frequently they have been nearly in a state of starvation. But such is the union and affection among them, and their love for this lonely Isle, that it is difficult to prevail on any of them to leave it. The appearance of the Island from the sea, as you approach it, is very beautiful. On the east and west, the rocks are lofty and mural; and a number of small rocks, a short distance from the Island, rise in curious pillars, arches, and lofty pyramids, over which, at certain tides, the sea breaks and foams in all its fury and grandeur.

As *we* came near, the Island seemed unapproachable, on account of its lofty mural sides and violent surges; but, passing between two of the rocky pillars, which stood only a few yards from each other, we entered a small bay, or bason, with a gravel beach. The inhabitants, who stood in groupes on the edge of the rocks, several hundred feet above the beach, came pouring down to give us a welcome.

There is a rugged path which winds among the rocks, and which leads to the extremity of a valley. About half a mie from this eastern extremity of the Island, are the cottages and cultivated ground, called the Town. To the West rises a lofty promontory, called Malcolm's Head; and on the N.E. the

Wart or Ward hill,* which is about 900 feet above the level of the sea; and on the S. E. is the small holm broken off from the Island, about a mile square, called the Sheep Craig, in which a number of sheep are annually fattened.

In the midst of the Island, is what is called, the churn; it is a hole, rather wider than a common well, through which you may see and hear the sea roll, although it is several hundred feet deep; and there is a cavern which extends under the Island as far as the churn; and persons have ventured in a boat until they could see the light coming through the churn into the cavern below.

The sea, in another place, has broken through the west promontory; and there is a pool of sea water, some distance inland, which is forced through these holes, called the holes of Keva.

Some of the stone in this Island is so fine, that hones are made of it, which give a fine edge to a razor. The boats in which they fish are very small and frail, of the canoe form. The Island affords no safe anchorage for vessels. The wreck of the formidable is yet to be seen east, close to the landing place. This was the flag ship of the Spanish Armada, which was wrecked on this Island, in 1588, when Duke de Medina Sidonia was attempting to sail back to Spain, by the north of the Orkneys. The Duke, with many of his crew, was saved, and after many difficulties he reached the Mainland of Shetland, and was conveyed by one of the Lairds to Holland.

There is a kirk, and schoolhouse in the Island, and they have a regular schoolmaster. The minister should visit them from Dunrossness once a year, but he is now infirm, and they are not visited by him for years. The Wesleyan ministers, from Lerwick, visit it once or twice a year, as the season permits. There are about fifty members in the Methodist society, and two leaders who hold religious meetings every Sabbath. Brand, who visited these Islands in 1700, says there were then only ten or twelve families in it; but that shortly after, the

---

* In every Isle there is a War, or Ward hill, the highest in the Island, where there was a watch kept, and they used to kindle a fire to apprise of an enemy; and now called a beacon.

small pox so raged, that it swept away two thirds of them; so
that there was not a sufficient number left to manage their
boats. They were, formerly, great smugglers, and also they
had remarkably good fishings. But, with all their nefarious
traffic, they are the poorest people in the whole of the Orkneys
and Shetland; and their fishings, for the last few years, have so
failed, and the seas become so rough, that unless things
greatly alter, it must be nearly deserted. I was much affected
to see so many beautiful young people imprisoned in this sea
girt Isle, beyond which they never go, and with so few com-
forts. On the morning I left, I baptized seven lovely
infants.

THE ISLAND OF FOULA.—Foula lies about thirty miles
N. W. from the Fair Isle, in the Atlantic ocean; about twenty
miles west of the centre of the Mainland. It is difficult to say
from what it derives its name. In some charts it is called
Foul Island, in opposition to ' Fair,' to which it is next; others
think it is taken from the vast number of fowls which inhabit
the Island. Dr. Clarke thinks this Island was the Thule of
the ancients, and it may be a corruption of the word Thule or
Thula.

It consists of three hills; the highest in the middle, is rather
conical and very lofty; it is about three miles long, and half that
broad. There are upwards of sixty merks of corn land, and
about two hundred inhabitants. The hills afford good pasturage for sheep and cows. The east side is much lower than the
west. The cliffs are very magnificent Lorafield—the highest is
about 1100 feet above the level of the sea. It is composed of
primitive rock, *i.e.* Granite Micacious and Quartz. Small
and sequestered as this Island is, it was, formerly, a place of
great religious privilege and literature. There is a place in it
now termed the Friars, and from the relics which have been
found, and some ancient records, it is very probable there were
a Monastery and College in Foula; and that Foula was in the
north Islands, what Jona was in the western.

There is but one landing place in this Island, so that it can
only be approached when there are favourable winds and tides.

There is much swell in the ocean between it and the mainland, which makes it dangerous to cross; yet I only heard of one boat being lost, which took place in the spring of 1834; by which five men and one woman were drowned; and three sisters, in one house, were left widows.

The inhabitants of this Island, formerly, were considered the best climbers of the rocks in Shetland; and many of the inhabitants were lost in their daring endeavours to catch the fowls which were very numerous, for the sake of their feathers, and the obtaining of their eggs.

The manner of catching them, and the great danger of it, are very well described by Miss Chalmers, a native poetess.

> " O scale the dangerous cliff no more,
> Above you, frowns the nodding steep;
> Below, the threatening billows roar;
> One moment gives you to the deep!
>
> O say, can nestled eggs or down,
> The uncertain objects of the strife,
> In the unequal balance thrown,
> One moment weigh against your life!
>
> In slender cord, on slender hold,
> Why life and safety will you trust!
> Son, Father, Husband, why so bold!
> Be to thyself, thy friends, more just.
>
> Why intrepidity debase!
> The cord may break, the hold give way,
> Nay, see! the faithless rock, alas!
> Time worn, in evil hour, decay.
>
> He sinks, he falls, to rise no more,
> Dashed on the rugged flint beneath;
> While we the spectacle deplore,
> It makes the wave a gentle death."

The Island belongs to Mr. Scott of Vaila, and to the ministry and parish of Walls; from the minister of which they receive an annual visit; and Mr. Peterson, a lay minister among the Independents, who is employed in the Island in the fishing season, frequently preaches to them. There is also a Wesleyan Methodist society, and they are visited by the minister of that denomination, from the Walls and Sandness circuit. Dr. Clarke visited this Island when he last visited Shetland, and laid the foundation stone for a chapel, in the most solemn manner; but on account of the Doctor's death, the chapel has not been built.

THE BURRA ISLES are near to the Mainland, only separated from the western cliffs of Coningsburgh, by a long narrow sound, a few hundred yards wide, called Cliff sound. The Islands are divided also by another narrow sound, which, in one place, is so narrow, that a rude kind of bridge is thrown over it, and unites the two Islands together. They are called east and west Burra. The east Island, which lies nearest the Mainland, is frequently called the Island of House, because there is an aule house upon it, in which resides the daughter of the old Laird, now Mrs. Webster.

It is probable they took their name from some Brough which stood upon them. West Burra, the largest Island, is about four miles long. There are about 300 merks of the best land in these Islands, of any in Shetland, and they are well situated for fishing, and contain five or six hundred inhabitants. There was formerly in West Burra, a Romish church called St. Laurence's, which had a lofty spire, and was an useful sea mark. It was one of three, built by three Norwegian sisters; one at Tingwall on the Mainland; another on a promontory called Ireland, on the Mainland near Bigton; and this in west Burra. Brand calls them Tower churches, which could give *advertisements* from one to the other.

But they have long since been demolished. The one in Burra was taken down to supply materials for building the present kirk. These Islands belong to Mr. Scott, the Laird of Scalloway, and a number of small Islands situated north and south of the Burras. Havery a fine grass Island with a few families upon it; *Papa* and *Oxna*, and a few other uninhabited Islands.

These Islands, formerly, belonged to the ministry of Brassay, but are now connected with a kirk at Quarf, on the west of the Mainland, in which he preaches alternately, when the weather permits. There are a good kirk and school house, and also a Methodist chapel and society, belonging to the Lerwick circuit.

TRONDRA is a small Island, laying east of the north end of West Burra, as it were, broken off from the north end of East Burra, from which it is divided by a voe, or arm of the sea, a few hundred yards wide. The north end of Trondra runs near to Scalloway, and forms part of Scalloway harbour. It is about a mile square, belonging to Lord Dundas: there are six or seven families upon it: it is in the parish of Tingwall. There is a school house, in which the Wesleyan ministers occasionally preach.

PAPA STOUR.—This Island lies opposite Sandness, just entering St. Magnus bay, considerably more north than the Islands last described. It is separated from the Mainland by a very rapid current, upwards of a mile wide; but it has four good harbours, one to the south, two to the north, and one to the west: nigh to this Island are the Lyra Skerries.

It is said the Island was anciently called *Stour* (large); but some Irish priests, celebrated for their sanctity, taking up their residence in this Island, it was called 'Papa Stour,' or 'the Stour of the Fathers.'

It is about three miles long, and two broad, and very fertile and interesting, containing 227 merks of rental land, and 350 inhabitants. This Island, in summer, is very romantic. There are, around it, many stupendous arches, and grand pillars, which fill the mind with sublime emotions of wonder and awe. There are several caves in Papa, into several of which boats can enter, and proceed many hundred feet, in which great numbers of seals are caught. There are many interesting Geological specimens to be found here. Jameson mentions some precious stones, porphyry, veins of green stone, basalt, and of stetile, in which latter are engrafted small masses of chalcedony and jasper. This is the Island on which the Hon.

Mr. Lindsey, brother to Lord Balcares, was, for upwards of twenty years *confined;* and from which he has lately been rescued. The greater part of the Island belongs to Lord Dundas; the other part to the Laird of *Buster*. Mr. Henderson, an hospitable man, lives in the Island, in an aule house; being, I believe, a taxman to Lord Dundas.

There is a kirk, which is connected with the ministry of Walls; and a Methodist chapel, built by an English lady, and called Hariot* chapel; and a small society, which is visited monthly, by the Wesleyan Ministers from Walls.

MUCKLE ROOE is the most northern Island of importance that I shall mention, on the west side of the Mainland; it is eight miles long, and two broad. It is divided only by a sound a few hundred yards across; at low water, it is so shallow, it is said, persons may wade over. The side next to the Mainland is low, but the west, which is exposed to the Atlantic is more elevated and rugged. At the south end of it, in Olnafirth voe, there are a few small grazing Islands. Vermantry, Oxney, Papa Little, Hildisha, &c. Muckle Rooe contains about 200 inhabitants, and is in the parish of Delting.

UNST is the most northern Island of the groupe, and extends nearly to sixty-two degrees north latitude. It is divided from the Island of Yell, by Blomel sound, which is very rapid and dangerous, and about half a mile wide.

It is nine miles long and four broad. It is reckoned one of the pleasantest Islands in the groupe; it is neither so boggy, nor hea:thy, as many of the other Islands. There is a considerable quantity of grass and corn land. It has three good harbours for vessels. Uyea sound, Balta sound, and Burra Firth. The sea coast, as in most other Islands, is rugged, and the Island mountainous. The principal hills are Valyfield, Crucyfield, and Vordhill. Valyfield, the highest is about 700 feet above the level of the sea. There are several fresh water lochs interspersed among the hills. It contains near 3000 merks of rental land, and about that number of inhabitants.

There are several things, in this Island, that would please the

* After the NAME of the Lady at whose expence it was built.

antiquarian. On the east side of the Island, are the ruins of Munus Castle, said to be built in 1598, by a Laurence Bruce, who came from Perthshire, and acquired a large estate, by purchasing land from the Norwegian Udallers. The following is over the gate :—

> " List ye to knaw this building quha began ?
> Laurence of Bruce, he was that worthy man.
> Quha earnestly his ayris and offspring prayes
> To help, and not to hurt—this work alwayes."

There are several large, rough stones, ten or twelve feet high, set up in various parts of the Island, intended as monuments to mark the site of some battle, or the grave of some chief. There are the remains of a Tumuli, called Harold's tomb, and a wick, called Harold's wick, where it is said King Harold landed, when he came from Norway, to subdue the pirates.

It cannot be the tomb of Harold, but one he might build for one of his chiefs; or some other, of that name.

On Crucyfield are circular ranges of stones, the remains, most probably, of a Scandinavian Temple, that was once sacred to the rights of the Deities of the Edda ; and in which, it is not unlikely, they held courts of judicature.

There are, also, the ruins of twenty-four Romish chapels. Some of the ruins still retain the names of the saints to whom they were dedicated. The ruins of several Pictish Burghs still remain. The Geology of this Island is very interesting ; fine specimens of serpentine-asbistos, magnesia, fossils ; and Dr. Hibert found great quantities of the cromate of iron, which is valuable.

There are several natural curiosities in this Island. Near Norwick is a place called ' Saxes Kettle,' from the sea rushing up through a narrow aperture, which causes it to boil with great violence. The legend of the country says, a giant used to boil his prey here ; and a famous well where they say their ancestors used to get boiled fish.

There are two kinds of eagles which reside on the hills and

H

bold sea precipices; and flocks of wild swans visit this Island, in autumn, in their migrations to warmer climes, and many are shot, for the sake of their down. The manners of the people are said to be more simple and primitive, than in any of the other Islands. The Norse language was spoken in this Island within the last sixty years. The population is scattered over the Island, but there are a good many respectable houses, and a shop at Uyea sound; and at Balta sound there are several respectable families, and some modern built houses. There used, says Brand, to be three kirks in this Island, forming one parish and ministry; but now, there is only one, an excellent new kirk: but it is far too distant from many parts of the Island. There is a respectable grammar school, the master of which, is the son of the minister, the Rev. William Ingram.

The Wesleyans preach in Colveydale, Uyea, and Under-Yule, &c.; and they have a good chapel in Norwick. There is also a small Independent chapel, near the Wesleyan chapel, visited monthly by the ministers from Yell.

Scaw is the last town in her majesty's dominions; I may say, the last town in the world, in this longitude.

I, therefore, went and stood upon the verge of this green earth, (for there is no land beyond this to the North Pole;) and as I looked towards the north, my imagination seemed desirous to brood over a *scene* so *vast*, *silent*, and *solitary*.

The small Island of *Uyea* is situated between Unst and Fetlar; south west of Unst, and North west of Fetlar; forming part of and giving the name to Uyea Sound; it is about a mile and a half long, and has several pleasant holms belonging to it. Mr. Leisk is the proprietor of the Island, I believe, and lives upon it, and also a family or two in his employ. The butter and cheese from this Island are most excellent for Shetland. Brand mentions a metal, having the colour of gold, which is found in great plenty in this Island, which some of the Dutch merchants took with them to Hamburgh, and tried it; but by the force of fire it did not melt, but crumbled into small peices.

There was an ancient Tumuli, or Burrow, opened in this

Island, and an urn full of bones found, which is now in the possession of Mr. Leisk.

The Island of *Fetlar* lies about three miles south of Unst, and about twelve miles north east of the Mainland. The surface of the earth is much the same as Unst, hard, and tolerably fertile; but not so lofty. It is five miles long, and four broad. It contains about 800 merks of rental land. There are a kirk, a manse, and school house in this Island, and a minister resides in it; but it is connected with another kirk in the north of Yell, so that in the parish there are about 1350 inhabitants; between six and seven hundred of which, I think, reside on this small Island. There are a Wesleyan society and chapel in this Island, which forms part of the Yell circuit. This Island is honoured by the residence of a Baronet, the only one in Shetland, Sir Arthur Nicholson. There are here also, the ruins of a Pagan Temple, a chalybeate spring, and some fine specimens of copper, iron, Plumbago rock, crystals, and fullers earth; but it is wanting of a good harbour.

YELL.—This Island is the largest of the groupe, except the Mainland. It lies south of Unst, and between *Fetlar* and the *Mainland;* from both which it is separated by rapid and dangerous sounds, several miles across, and which, in winter, are frequently impassable for weeks together. It lies about twenty-four miles N. E. from Lerwick. The extent of it is variously stated. I think it is about twenty miles long, and six or seven broad.

It is divided into three parishes; South Yell, Mid Yell, and North Yell. It is the least fertile, and most thinly populated, of any of these Islands.

In the ministry of Mid Yell, which includes South Yell, there are between fourteen and fifteen hundred inhabitants; and about seven or eight hundred in North Yell. At the south end of Yell are two good, but not commodious harbours; Hamna voe, and a little east of this, *Burra voe;* so called, from having a brough near it, the ruins of which yet remain.

On the west side of this voe, the land is tolerably cultivated, and there is a considerable number of inhabitants. Close to the side of the voe is the residence of Robert Bruce, the Laird of Burra Voe; and at the head of the voe is the Wesleyan chapel, and the minister's house. The situation is very romantic, but the house is too small for a family, as it was originally intended only for a single man. The east coast which divides the sea from the voe by a narrow tongue of land, is rocky and shattered; and when there is a storm from the east, the mountain billows which break over them are amazing; the spray of which, at times, comes over the chapel and house, into the voe.

Behind the chapel is one of the loftiest and most singular rocks in the Island, called the 'Horse of Burra,' under which are several extensive caverns, which are entered from the east sea. I visited some of them. The swell of the sea was so great, we could not enter the first we attempted; but we rowed a good way up several others, which gradually became lower and darker, except one; as we advanced, we saw the light coming from a cavern on the other side. The silence and solitude were impressive, which were interrupted occasionally by the droppings of water from the top, the booming occasioned by the swell of the sea, the sudden flight of sea fowl, or the snorting of seals.

The water was wonderfully transparent; through which, we could see the rocks beneath us, of various fantastic forms, and a number of weeds and shells, of various colours; but the whole was slightly tinged with green, forming a beautiful submarine picture.

On coming out, the rocks over our heads appeared vast and terrific; about which a number of sea fowls are constantly hovering.

The eagle here builds her nest, which she just left as we came out of the cavern, and soared with no middle flight.

Beyond Burra voe, about two miles north, is Gossaburgh; the way to which is wild, and barren, and interspersed with lochs, morasses, and peat pits. The cottages are built around the head of a fine bay; and there is a good aule house, with some tolerably good grass and corn land.

The former Laird of this property, was a Mr. Basil Robertson; but now a Mr. John Ogilvey, who married his daughter.

A little beyond this is Swarrister, which is much of the same description as Gossaburgh. Midyell lies from hence five miles north and by west, over a trackless waste, so full of *burns* and *braes* and morasses, as not only to make it difficult, but even dangerous to travel alone.

Mid Yell harbour is completely land locked, and is formed by a voe winding inland some miles. Around this harbour are several merchants houses, and a modern built kirk, and *manse*, and several groupes of cottages. The school house, they told me, was at an inconvenient distance, and they were then without a schoolmaster. Mid Yell is becoming an important station for the herring fishing. About two miles north east from hence is Basta voe, about which there is a good deal of cultivated land on both sides of the voe, and on the north side of Sella Firth. There are two good houses in this vicinity, one at the head of Basta Voe, and the other at the head of Sella Firth. About half a mile east from the mouth of this voe, is a small town called Burraness, and receives its name from its situation on a ness, and because it is the situation of a brough, or ancient castle, which is still in a great state of preservation. Two miles beyond this, opposite to Gillivoe, stands the kirk of North Yell. The North end of Yell is far the best part of the Island, containing several good wealthy families and cultivated ground. The north west scenery of Yell is the most romantic, having several bold promontories and rugged cliffs. Mr. John Ogilvey has a beautiful mansion at West Sandwick; from whence, on the way to Hamna voe, we leave on the right Haverie sound, Scetur, Ulster, and Coppister; the way is wild and trackless. At Hamna voe, formerly, stood the South Yell kirk, which is now in ruins. The minister has now no where to preach, except in a private house, or the Methodist chapel. The Wesleyans have six or seven societies, consisting of about one hundred members, in this Island. There were formerly twenty Roman Catholic chapels in this Island: but there are the ruins of one only to be seen, which is on the Island of Hascosea, opposite to the mouth of Mid Yell voe.

The rocks are, generally, composed of granite, micacious,

shastus, and quartz. To the east side of Yell, is the Isle of
Hascosea, two miles long: to the south, the Isle of Samphra,
one mile long: to the south west, the Isle of Biga, a mile and
a half long: all pleasant and good grazing Isles; with a *few*
inhabitants in each of them, as they are well situated for fishing:
for if the wind blow from the west, the boats can lay on the
east; and if from the east, they can lay on the west.

THE ISLAND OF WHALSEY lies south east from Yell and
east by north from Lerwick; across a sound of twelve miles;
but it is not more than three miles from the nearest point of
the Mainland; it is four miles long, by three miles wide. The
Island rises in the centre rather conically, and gradually declines
to its extremities both north and south; but the scenery, generally, is not very bold and romantic. This is the residence of
Mr. Bruce of Sembister, one of the principal Lairds in Shetland.
He has lately built a very costly mansion on the Island, all
of granite, which the people commonly call the palace. There
are upon the Island about 700 inhabitants, and many hundred
merks of rental land. It is connected with the ministry of
Nesting. Beyond Whalsey, about twelve miles east, are the
out Skerries, consisting of three Islands, which form a triangle;
the whole of them being scarcely a mile in length. The rocks
around these skerries, are perpendicular and rather lofty;
except the south east and the east, which is the entrance into a
fine little harbour. The part which is cultivated, forms a kind
of amphitheatre, or basin, and is so concealed that you would
really think you were on a much larger Island. There are
nine houses and about ninety inhabitants. There is a kirk on
the middle Island, which is occasionally preached in by the
minister from Nesting, and the Wesleyan ministers from the
Yell circuit. But being so small, and surrounded by such
boisterous seas that the spray beats over the Islands, and frequently destroys their crops. These Islands form a fishing
station of considerable importance, both for the long line, and
early herring fishing. Men, from different Islands, live here
for several months during the fishing season, in temporary sod
huts and booths. At the south end of the middle Island, there

is a remarkable cave, that is said will contain a hundred men, and yet only one can enter at once; in which, men have at times, concealed themselves from the press gang. In summer, these Islands are very pleasant and tranquil; but viewing them from the Mainland, they appear dreary and desolate. The people live harmoniously; they appear to be all of one family, and are not only contented, but even delighted, with these remote and sequestered dwellings.

The Skerries, and the greater part of the Islands of Whalsey, belong to Mr. Bruce; and the other part to Mr. Hay. One great inconveniency is, they have no peats here, but have to fetch them from Whalsey. It was on these skerries that the Carmelan of Amsterdam was wrecked in 1664, containing much gold.

The Island of Brassa is east of the Mainland, just opposite Lerwick; and forms the eastern shore of Brassa sound, a spacious and safe harbour, which has given such a superiority to Lerwick, on account of the ships coming to and from these Islands. This Island is about five miles long, and two and a half broad; it is very irregular in its shape. To the south east, it rises in a conical lofty mountain, upwards of 600 feet above the level of the sea, called the whart; at the top of which, is built a tower of loose stones, from which may be seen all the remote Islands, and a great part of the Mainland; and the sea nearly all around. The shore of the harbour is low, but it gradually rises to the south east, where the rocks become perpendicular. The highest promontory at the south east is called the Bard, about 900 feet high. Sailing round, at the south east end of the Island, from the sea may be seen many curious pillars, arches, and caverns. It contains about 700 inhabitants, and 300 merks of rental land. In this Island there are the ruins of several ancient chapels. This Island belongs to Wm. Mouat McLean, Esq., who has a summer mansion there called Gardie. The mansion is very ancient, and the gardens and land around it, in a high and superior state of cultivation. In one of the gardens is a hot house, in which grapes and peaches are brought to astonishing perfection. In this Island, also, there are the tombs of several Scandinavian chiefs. There is a standing stone, a kind of monument, of ancient date, the history of which is wrapt in a deal of obscurity.

Noss.—On the south east side of Brassa is the small but fertile Island of Noss, which is separated from Brassa by a narrow strait, only a few hundred feet across. The Island is a fine pasturage for milch cows. There is but one house in the Island, near which are the ruins of an old kirk; the burying ground still remains, in which there are a considerable number of grave stones, and grave boards still standing. At the east end of the Island, is a remarkable holm, separated from the Island about 240 feet; and though not 200 feet in height, yet being on all sides perpendicular and surrounded by the sea, one would have thought these sufficient obstacles to have made it inaccessible. But, no—a man was employed to climb this rock, and to drive in stakes, to which, strong ropes were fastened and thrown over to the Island, and were fastened by stakes; and a wooden box, called the cradle, made to slide over the ropes, to and from the holm; but the person in returning, fell and was dashed in pieces. The cradle is now commonly used for going over to the holm to gather eggs, and to catch sea fowl: they also take sheep over in it, to feed in the holm, during the winter; and the next summer they take them out fat. Above this rises what is called the Noup of Noss, which is a perpendicular rock, six or seven hundred feet above the level of the sea; on which, numbers of sea fowl build, and perch; and if anything be thrown down the face of the rock, so as to alarm them, the number of birds which fly out, and the noise they make, would astonish you. The noup is known, by sea men, as a land mark, called Hang Cliff, by which they make observations in coming north or east.

Mousa, or Queen's Island, is situated near the south end of the Mainland, east; but there is only a sound of a few hundred yards between it and the Mainland. It is twelve miles below Lerwick, a mile long, and near half a mile broad.

There are two houses upon the Island; the house in which Mrs. Piper resides, who is the widow of the late proprietor;

and a cottage for the shepherd.   There is a small piece of corn land; but it may be considered as a grazing Isle, for about sixty cows, and two hundred sheep are kept upon it.   It is now in the possession of Mr. Yorston, banker, Lerwick.   In this Island there is a Brough, which is said to be the most perfect of any in Europe.   This Brough was in ruins in the twelfth century; for when Earland fled from Orkney to Shetland, with Margaret, the mother of Earl Ronald, her son, being opposed to the marriage, pursued them.   Earland took refuge in this Brough in Mousa, which he fortified, and was resolved to hold out to the last; but Ronald was at length prevailed upon, and consented to the marriage.   The present appearance of it is very curious; it is a round bulging tower, about forty feet high, and rather more than that round, built of stone, closely compacted without mortar, and grown over, in several parts with pale dry moss.   You enter on the west side by a low door; it is open at the top, and appears never to have been covered.   The walls are many yards thick, and the rooms are in the walls, which seem only adapted for security, or conceal-ment.   There is a winding staircase to the top of it, and in the walls there seems to be a labyrinth, in which a person, for a long time might evade the closest search.   It is the opinion of a certain writer, that they were also used as burying places for the great; and that our word ' burying' came from ' putting into a Burgh.'   This Island is not lofty, but you have a fine view from it of the broken rugged east coast of the Mainland.

THE MAINLAND.—The principal Island in this groupe is called the Mainland, as it is not only much larger than any other Island, but, I should think, larger than them all put together.   It is upwards of sixty-five miles in length, and varies in breadth from three to twelve miles.

The length way of the Island is nearly north and south, and the breadth east and west.   But it is so intersected with the sea, that you can never be more than three miles, at any place, from some arm of it.

Lerwick, which is the capital, or, I might say, the only town in the Islands, is situated on the east coast, about the centre of

I

the Mainland, rather nearer to the southern extremity. It has risen to its present superiority, through the excellency of its situation and harbour.

It is, comparatively, a modern built town. Scalloway on the western shore, about five miles from this, was the ancient capital.

In 1633, when Captain Smith visited Shetland, the town of Lerwick was not in existence, or not of importance to excite attention. It was an inconsiderable place until about the end of the seventeenth century; when, for the conveniency of trafficking with Dutch fishing vessels, which at that time were about two thousand annually, it rapidly increased, until in 1809, Dr. Edmonstone stated the population at 1600, and at present it contains about three thousand inhabitants.

When Brand visited these Islands in A.D. 1700. the population was between two and three hundred families. They had then built a kirk, but they belonged to Tingwall parish, or ministry, had no minister settled among them, and enjoyed the means of grace but seldom; therefore, they then made application to government to have some allowance out of the revenues of the bishoprick of Orkney, or otherwise, as the wisdom of government should see meet, so that there might be a competency made up for the ministers stipend; they also exerting their ability; and also, requesting the general assembly to erect the town into a parish. For, says Brand, the want of ordinances maketh their case very sad and deplorable; it nurseth ignorance, occasioneth much sin, especially horrid profanation of the Lord's Day, by strangers as well as by inhabitants; and doth effectually obstruct the conversion of souls, the preaching of the word being the special means of convincing and converting sinners, and building them up in holiness, and comfort, through Faith unto Salvation.

In 1733, when Gifford wrote his description of Zetland, it appears in a lower state than in the time of Brand; not above two hundred families, and the trade declining.

The town of Lerwick consists of one principal street, which runs close round the shore of the harbour, and if not so irregular, and ill planned, would something resemble a crescent. The sea washes the foundations at the back of the N.E. side of the street, the front of which is S.W.   The S.W. side of the street is a short distance from the sea, and faces towards the harbour and Brassa.   The street is without any plan, some of the houses fronting, others have their gables towards the street, and frequently protruding many feet out of the line, and nearly every house on a different model, without order or uniformity. But if a few of the most offensive things to good taste were removed, it would much improve the town; especially, a place called the Trance, where the street becomes much interrupted by two gables, from the opposite sides of the street, meeting within about four or five feet, and a room being thrown over the top.   The street is paved with flag stones, but now is considerably out of repair.

This street consists principally of shops, which are termed by the people 'merchants,' but what in England would be called 'shopkeepers.'   They are a kind of general dealers, and most of them sell bottled ale, porter, and whiskey.   There are a few who may be called merchants, who keep vessels, and trade with foreign ports.   But Mr. Hay and Mr. Ogilvey are the principal merchants and bankers in Lerwick. They are men of great respectability, and considerable wealth, and, to all appearance, they are doing much to improve the Islands, and benefit the people.   Several of the most respectable shopkeepers have formed themselves into a shipping company.   They have one vessel constantly trading between Lerwick and Leith, called the Magnus Triol, a fine sailing schooner.   The principal managers of which, are Mr. Goston, banker; Mr. Gaven Gaudy; Mr. James Hunter; Mr. Malcolm and Robert Sinclairs; Mr. Laurenson, &c.   In this street is the Tollbooth, which contains the prison, and court house, and the Free Masons lodge, a large room, in which public lectures are sometimes delivered.   There are two public libraries, containing seven or eight hundred volumes each, as far as I can remember.

From this main street, a number of narrow lanes branch out, called closes, rising up to the south west.   Several of them are exceedingly steep, narrow, and irregular, wet, and unpaved; with houses only here and there, interspersed with small patches of enclosed ground. If indeed the whole town had been promiscuously thrown together, it could not have been much more destitute of order. Many of the houses, in these closes, are very wretched, dirty, smoky places, and let out in single rooms to the poor, and labouring classes. There are the south kirk close, and the north kirk close; in a space, in the midst of these two closes, stands the old kirk, which is now converted into assembly rooms, and a much more commodious new kirk is built, at the top of the north kirk close. But the burying ground connected with the old kirk still continues, the only one for the town; in which there is a considerable number of tombs and grave stones. But they have now walled in a piece of ground above the new kirk for a cemetry which is very tastefully laid out.

The third close is called Bakers close, on account of the only baker in the Islands residing in it. The public well which supplies the town and the shipping is in this close. It was very primitive and curious, when I first came to the Island, but lately, they have placed over it a public pump, which is frequently, in summer, locked up only at certain hours, which, frequently makes a great crowd, by persons waiting for their turn. About half way up this close stands the Wesleyan chapel, a small, neat, white building, fronting the harbour. It was built in 1824. It will seat upwards of threee hundred, and is capable of receiving a gallery, which is very desirable. The preachers house is built at the back of the chapel, fronting the south-west, and looking over the land. It is a large, good house, containing six rooms, but has no ground or garden connected with it. It is called the *Mission* house, as the preachers going from, and coming to, the Islands with their families, stay with the minister residing here, sometimes for several weeks; and also at the district meeting, the whole of the preachers are, generally, accommodated at the Mission house. These premises were built during the superintendence of **Mr.** Lewis, and under the auspices of Mr. Samuel Dunn.

There are several more closes north of this. At the top of these closes there are two roads, one runs from 'east to west, and the other from south to north, forming an angle. In the first stands the new parish kirk, a good, substantial, and (in the inside,) elegant church, that will seat upwards of 1000 hearers. Just opposite which stand Mr. Spence's cottage and surgery; and the custom house, in which Mr. Fea, the commissioner, resides. A road passes the Custom house, and west of the kirk, to the Knab, which is the extremity of the harbour, south; a headland, broken, and mural, from which it is awful to look down into the chasm or yawning deep below. From the Knab you have a fine view of vessels approaching within sight of the Islands, from the south. The end of the Island of Brassa on the east, and the Knab on the west, form the mouth of the harbour, which is several hundred yards across. On the west side of the road that leads to the knab, is the town house of —— Mouat, Esq., Laird of Garth; it is called Annesbray. In the front of the house is a large grass plot, and two small wings at the end of the palisade in front; in the one next the kirk, lives Mr. John Smith, who, a short time since, was the only respectable shoemaker in the town; but lately several others have commenced. In this street, more west, stands the Independent chapel, which, I think, will hold more than the Wesleyan chapel. But being small, and the galleries large, it looks dark and crowded. The congregation is tolerable, the minister aged and infirm, but a peaceable and pious man. They are the followers of Aldine, and take the sacrament weekly. Just opposite this chapel is the grammar, or free school for the parish. The schoolmaster is the son of a respectable surgeon in Lerwick, and nephew of the minister of the parish, Mr. Barclay. There is another school, in which the sons of the more opulent are educated in the classics, &c., by a Mr. Martin, an Englishman.

The road, running north, has several good houses fronting the west, or south, with the gables west. Mr. Brand's, Lieutenant of the Coast Gaurd; Mr. A. Duncan's, writer, son to the sheriff; Mr. Duncan's, brother to the sheriff, writer; Mr. Reed's, Inde-

pendent minister; and a good many other small houses, in front
of which, are several small paddocks and gardens enclosed.
The road leads to the docks, which are north of the fort. The
docks are the private property of Messrs. Hay and Ogilvey. It
is a place of great extent and business for Shetland. Here is
the principal fishing station in the Islands, and great numbers
of coopers are employed in making herring barrels. Boat and
ship building is going on; sawyers, smiths, masons, &c., are
busy; vessels and boats loading and unloading; indeed, the
business done here, in a good fishing season, is astonishing.

A little south of this is the garrison, called fort Charlotte, a
small fort strongly walled round, shut in with gates, and mounted
by twelve pieces of cannon. The barracks in the fort are sufficient for a regiment of foot soldiers; but their are but one or
two kept now, to open and shut the gates, and take care of the
cannon. The officers apartments are let to Dr. Edmonstone, a
physician; and to Misses Campbell, who teach a school of
young ladies.

Brand says, this citadel was built in the time of the Dutch
war, A.D. 1665, by workmen sent by authority from Scotland;
but the work was never perfected, the men returning home in
A.D. 1667. At that time three hundred soldiers were sent over
for the defence of the Islands against the hostile incursions of
the Dutch. The garrison could do much to command the
harbour, (for then there was no town here.) The walls are yet in
good condition, high in some places without, but filled up with
earth within. There hath been a sally port, dangerous to
attack, by reason of a deep ditch before it, fed by a spring;
into which, by the stratagems of war, the enemy might be led
and sink. But the barracks were burnt down by the Dutch
after our soldiers had left the fort. This fort was again repaired in the reign of George the Third, and called 'Fort
Charlotte,' after his Queen. It is the most northern fort in the
empire, and gives rather a military aspect to the town.

Lerwick is almost entirely surrounded by the sea, so that it
would have been cut off from the Mainland, and formed a small
Island, but a few yards or little more than the breadth of three

roads; one between the sea and a loch of fresh water, west; another road north, at the end of this loch; and then there is another fresh water loch, at the end of which there is the third narrow space between the loch and the sea. On the first loch, in the centre, are the ruins of a large Picts Castle. It appears at a distance, merely a vast mass of stones. But if you pass over some stepping stones placed in the water, and inspect it, the inside is round and like an amphitheatre; and in the walls, near the ground, are small rooms. It must have been similar when perfect, I think, to the one in Mousa.

Lerwick is much improving; several of the inhabitants of late, have been over to Scotland, and learned trades, and have lately set up in business. A plumber and glazier, joiner and painter, and several tradesmen have come over from Scotland. There are several medical men and two druggist's shops; and an inn just commenced, but I could find no hair dresser.

There is no market, so that the supplies are irregular and precarious, and no fresh meat, at times, for months. Many improvements might be made in Lerwick, by way of paving, lighting, and cleaning, the town; which, I doubt not, will in time take place.

The scenery in the vicinity of Lerwick has but little to recommend it. In many other parts of the Island it is much more wild and lofty, or level and cultivated.

The Sound of Lerwick is the only interesting part in the vicinity. From the town to the sound is about half a mile, on the west road, which is the road that leads out of town to every part of the Island. To the right, about half way between Lerwick and the sound, is Mr. Hay's farm, which is a genteel house two stories high, with a garden in front, surrounded by high walls, for the security of a few fruit trees which are growing in the garden. There are several paddocks behind Mr. Hay's farm, which have been delved and drained, and which look like little Goshens, fruitful and fair, when contrasted with the rocky, uneven, barren land around. The road from Mr. Hay's farm to the sound is sufficiently wide and level for gigs to run upon; for several of the gentlemen keep gigs for a pony to drive them to and from the town. There are two or three detached houses on each side the road. Just beyond Cleckern Inn, (a cottage where ponies are let out for hire,) the road runs over a narrow neck of land, between an arm of the sea and a fresh water loch, and winds round, for a short distance, by the side of the sea; and then, leaving the sea side a short distance, you come to the sound.

It is a tongue of land running into the sea, having the sea on the south, east, and west. Several Lerwick gentlemen have built here country houses, where they reside in summer; Mr. Yorston, banker; Mr. Greig, procurator fischal; and Mr. Fea, Commissioner of Customs; they are neat small places.

Mr. Ogilvey, merchant and banker, has built an elegant villa. He has literally turned the wilderness into a fruitful field, and the desert into a garden. The fields are green, the gardens are extensive, planted with trees, and gravel walks, and a green-house well stocked with choice plants, flowers, &c. The difficulty and expence have been great, no doubt, as he has had to blow up the rock for some acres, and to delve and drain the whole, to build walls, and make roads, &c. On the west and north of the sound, there are a number of cottages, and a considerable quantity of cultivated ground; and at the foot of a range of high barren hills, north west of the loch, Mr. Laurence Duncan has built a neat house, where he constantly resides. On a calm day, as you pass on the road, you will see the hills and this and another house or two beautifully reflected from the loch, as from a mirror.

There is one thing more in the vicinity of Lerwick, which I shall briefly notice.

North of the town, about quarter of a mile beyond the docks, are several houses and some excellent corn land. There is a good white house, called Grimester, belonging to Sir Arthur Nicholson; but it is let to, and is now in the occupation of Mr. Mercless, the precentor at the kirk in Lerwick. The land around it is very boggy, and the hills covered with nothing but hether. A road, out by Grimester, was commenced, that would have been much more level and nearer for gigs to have driven on to Scalloway; but as it went through Sir Arthur's ground he forbad it, and so the road remains unfinished.

That I may give you a topographical view of the Mainland, the reader must accompany me on a tour to Dunrossness, south; and then to North Roe, which will take in the length of the Mainland; and then west to Scalloway, and north-west to Walls, which will take you across the breadth of the Mainland.

The first tour to Dunrossness which is twenty-five miles south. The road runs through Upper Sound, where there are about a dozen cottages. The cultivated land in the vicinity of Lerwick ends here, a sod wall running south and north, in which a gate is fixed to keep the cattle from coming off the scathold, or wilds, and injuring the corn. After you pass the gate, the road winds through an exceeding stony and useless piece of ground; a large burn runs down a rugged channel by the side of the road, which when swollen by rains, breaks and dashes along with noisy roar: at an angle in the road there is a small bridge built. The road now becomes much worse, and the land no better. Hills rise again from the top of this which are broken, rocky, and dark. The road passes between two lochs, one south and the other north, and in the midst of a number of peat pits. The road ends here, just before you come to the top of Stunken hill, in two branches; one intended to have been carried on to Scalloway, and the other to Dunrossness, but they have not been extended for some years. From the top of Stunken hill over waving and rugged headlands, the sea view south east is vast. You see east, the most lofty southern extremity of the Island of Brassa; and to the west and south west, hills rising above hills, in all their native and dark sterility; but the valley just below is most fertile and beautiful, in which many cottages are scattered in various directions, called Gulberwick.

After you pass through this valley, the ground becomes broken and boggy. You pass west of Brimster, which consists of a few cottages, walled in with sods. A little west is a large loch surrounded by barren hills, which they cross to Sundabank. In this loch there are the remains of an old Picts Castle.

K

After passing a burn which runs from the loch into the sea below, a piece of road again commences and continues only for a few hundred yards, and then the way becomes broken, boggy and difficult to travel, until a small piece of road again appears which leads on to Quarf. At the top of the hill of Quarf, you have a fine view of two smooth, green, grassy hills, called Snuga and Scraffa, which sweep regularly and beautifully into the valley, which is extensive and well cultivated, and a number of *towns* as they call them, or groups of cottages in it. The kirk, an excellent new white building, and slated with blue slate, stands a few hundred yards from the road. It differs from nearly all the other kirks, it having a small steeple and a bell. Most of the country kirks are built just like an English barn, and about as well fitted up inside. The manse, or minister's house, stands a little way up the hill, built in the cottage style, being only one story high, but very neat, being white and slated with blue slate, containing four or five apartments, and a garden, and a few small paddocks around it. In summer, the scenery here may be called beautiful, for the greenness of the meadows, and the corn spangled with yellow flowers, and a large burn runs winding along the valley and empties itself into the east sea, just where the road passes over a gravelly bed. Quarf is five long miles from Lerwick, and about three from Coningsburgh. The valley is about two miles long, and takes in the whole width of the Mainland from east to west. As you ascend the hill south of Quarf, the road again commences as soon as you pass through the grind, or gate, of the sod wall. This road extends several miles; but a short distance from the east sea, after leaving Quarf, you soon come to Fladabister, or pass the outer wall leaving it to the east on the coast, which is low and broken, and the west hills close and high. It is a fine fertile valley, and has in it a number of cottages. There was formerly a Roman Catholic chapel here, but I can find no ruins of it; nothing but a hole called 'Kirk Hole.' The people believe it was here a church once stood. Formerly the road ended at Fladabister, but the last time I was here the road was making to Coningsburgh, as you wind round the foot of the hill from Fladabister to

Coningsburgh. The valley is open and spacious, a kind of amphitheatre, surrounded by hills; but this valley is without cultivation and full of peat pits. The first house you come to, before you cross a large burn, is the schoolmaster's, Mr. Goudie, who has much improved the land about his house. He is a fine old man, and his wife is very affectionate, and as far as they are able, they are very hospitable.

The name of this parish signifies "the King's Burgh, or City," and was perhaps, formerly, the most important part of the Island. Crossing the burn, you find a few cottages; and the Sheriff, a little beyond, has a small farm house: and having passed this and another house, you come to a valley well filled with cottages, surrounded by green meadows and a considerable quantity of cultivated land. Through these meadows run large and winding burns, which are exceedingly useful and beautiful as there are no rivers.

The cliffs of Coningsburgh are the loftiest and finest mountain scenery in the south of the Island. They are high and rugged; it may be said hills rise out of hills, or hills are piled one upon another; and the bare rocks jutting out and rising up here and there, seem to lay open, as it were, the foundations of the earth. The hills north west of the cliffs are wild and noble, trackless and houseless; but in the cliffs there are a few cottages, and over the greater part of the cliffs fine grass grows. The road winds along the middle of them, in some places hundreds of feet above the sea, and yet many hundreds from the top. The hills above and below the path, in spring are adorned with primroses, and deep yellow, blue, and scarlet wild flowers; and here and there, a few sheep are scattered, and some ranging on the highest cliffs. The shore is rocky, black, and shattered; a vast of sea weed, called Tang, grows upon the rocks and stones; and also much shell fish, so that you frequently see a number of men, women, and boys, getting the limpets for baits, and the tangle to burn for kelp, or spread on the ground for manure. Leaving the cliff, you enter through a gate in a stone wall, and enter Sandwick parish. The ground is unsound and boggy, but keeping east the road is better. The first group of houses in the parish is called *Setter*. To the east of which close under the hill on the shore, is Sand Lodge, the mansion of Mr. John Bruce, the Laird of Sumburgh. The house, gardens, and walled in grazing paddocks, or fields, have rather an imposing appearance. There are a number of cottages west of it. The remaining part of the south end of the Mainland is called the ' Mid Lothian of Shetland,' on account of its superior cultivation and fertility ; it is also much more thickly inhabited than the north part. In this parish there are a kirk, and manse, (or minister's house,) built in the cottage style. The cottages in this parish are the best I have seen. On the east coast are several bold promontories, and the Island of Mousa.

Hoswick, the name of a large group of houses, lies southwest from the kirk, near the shore of the bay of Lavenwick sound. Between the kirk and Hoswick stands the first Wesleyan chapel you meet with south of Lerwick. It is a plain barn like place, without any ceiling inside, open to the roof. It will contain upwards of two hundred hearers. The Wesleyan society here consists of five leaders, and upwards of eighty members.

From Hoswick to Sumburgh Head is about eleven miles, and fourteen from Lerwick. The Mainland here is so narrow, that after passing from Sandwick parish there is only one range of hills and small villages, on the east and west shores. On the west is *Bigtown, Ireland, Maywick, Rerwick,* and *Scosburgh;* on the east, is Levenwick ; to which, in fine weather, you may cross the sound from Hoswick to Levenwick, which is about half a mile across, and save much tiresome walking ; for to Levenwick by land is two miles. Over the high hill above Hoswick, you come to a few cottages called Shannorwick. The sea comes inland and rolls a mighty surge over a fine sand. When I passed over these sands in 1832, the skeletons of several several hundreds of whales lay bleaching on the sand. The road on the east passes the Mull, and winds on the edge of several precipitous rocks. Levenwick consists of a number of cottages grouped together and a few lone houses. From several bold promontories you have vast sea views. Gungster, a point of land running into the sea, is bold and rugged. A sailor, (belonging to an Archangel vessel that put into Levenwick sound, and was detained for some time,) was entertaining himself in catching birds on the crags of Gungster, when his foot slipping, he fell from the top of this promontory, which is awful to look down, and was dashed in pieces. His body was interred in a small burying ground, which strikes the attention, a small green elevated spot, surrounded by the loose sand of the beach; close up to which, at times, the sea rolls—here many a ship-wrecked seamen lies.

There are many frail memorials of the dead on small stones and peices of wood, on most of which are the initials of the persons buried there, and the age and dates, rudely cut, excepting two. The first was sacred to the memory of Marion Atkin, who was buried in the year 1822, aged 68; the widow of a drowned fisherman. The other recorded the deaths of a man and his wife, the wife's maiden name was Irvine, aged 70. The husband William Robertson, died aged 82. You may frequently see the mournful procession slowly moving over these dark and heath clad hills, or approaching the beach in boats.

In Levenwick there is a school house, but no school master. The Wesleyans visit this place from Lerwick monthly, and preach in the school house, which is generally full. There are twelve members in this society. Levenwick lies at the foot of a range of very high and steep hills west, and round a sandy bay from the top of the hills above Levenwick. The views are very extensive, especially to the west, where the Islands in the atlantic, and the blue distant peaks of Foula, are seen to great advantage.

From Levenwick to the parish church of Dunrossness is about four miles, but the road is difficult and dangerous without a guide, for a stranger on account of the burns, peat pits, and the number of large bogs. About half a mile from the kirk, the lofty hill of Scosburgh terminates rather abruptly; and a rather flat piece of ground, for several miles round, is thickly populated for Shetland.

Dunrossness parish. The *name* of the parish is a general

term used to designate all the places in the parish, but every little group of cottages has a particular name, and sometimes a single house or cottage. The parish kirk, and the Wesleyan and Baptish chapels, stand in a triangle, within the circle of a mile. They stand on small eminences, a short distance from any other building. Around the Wesleyan chapel the ground is uncommonly uneven, stony, and sterile, so that its first appearance is rather desolate. It is one of the largest and best chapels in the Island, and will seat about five hundred hearers, and has, what all the other chapels are destitute of, two or three small vestries, but the chapel, like the others, is unceiled. It was built during the superintendence of Mr. Tabraham.

The places of worship are well situated, in the midst of a considerable population for four miles round. The manse is in Skelberry; Voe, Clumble, and several other groups of cottages lie north east and south. Between the kirk and Sumburgh, which is about four miles, there are several towns which I shall mention in order. The view from the Wesleyan chapel is very interresting. On the east you can see the north sea stretching to the horizon; on the west, the atlantic; on the north, the hill of Scosburgh; on the south, hoary Fitfill rises in gloom. On a winter's night, when the chapel is lighted up, the effect upon the surrounding solitude and darkness, leads the mind to the declaration of the Prophet, " The wilderness and the solitary place shall be made glad because of him." There are eight class leaders in the Wesleyan society in Dunrossness, and about one hundred and seventy members. The chapel is visited by the ministers from Lerwick monthly. There are three or four school houses in this parish, but several of them are without regular masters. The Wesleyans have four or five scripture schools.

On the way to Sumburgh head you pass the residence of the Lady of Brough, as she is called, the widow of the Laird of Brow, a fine old woman, upwards of ninety years of age, with whom resides Mrs. Ogilvey, a widow lady, and the ladies grandson, and his wife and family. Mr. Cragie practises as a surgeon : he married the daughter of the late Dr. Ireland, of

North Leith. The grand daughter of the Lady of Brough, and sister of Mr. Cragie, is the wife of Mr. Grierson, the son of the old Laird of Quendal, the adjoining Lairdship; she is a very agreeable, talented, and pious lady. Brow is a house of call for most respectable persons travelling this way, to whom is shewn no little kindness. From the top of the hill above Brow to Virkie is a complete sandy desert; hundreds of acres, that once were fertile, have been deluged with sand, and in many places it is blown away to the naked rock. A wall has been built round a fine flat piece, of several acres, in hopes of rescuing it, but in many places the walls are completely buried in sand. There are two or three cottages and some few pieces of this light sandy land cultivated near a loch at Hardbreaks. The two last towns south are Enobie and Virkie. From Virkie to Sumburgh head is two miles.

At the south end of the Mainland are the two bold promontories called Sumburgh head, and Fitfill head. The former runs out into the sea much farther than the latter. Sumburgh is on the east side, and Fitfill on the west, around the bases of which rolls a heavy sea, and rapid currents sweep along with noisy roar. The name of the parish is taken from the din of the roost, formerly spelt Dyn Raust Ness. Between these two promontories is a bay called Quendal Bay, a good harbour to those who know its entrance, except with a south or south west wind. These two promontories are celebrated as the classic ground of Shetland. They are fixed upon as the places where the two principal characters resided, in Sir Walter Scott's novel of the Pirate; old Morton residing on Sumburgh head, and the witch Norna on Fitfill. Sumburgh head, though vast in bulk, is only about three hundred feet above the level of the sea, but steep and rugged all around except in one place, east. There has, within these last few years, been a lighthouse built upon its summit, consisting of two wings and a round tower in the middle. The two wings are houses for the manager and his assistant. The tower in the middle is about thirty-five feet high, and has a winding staircase to the top, where the lights are placed within a glass dome, the framework of which is strong cast iron, and the glass thick plate, to withstand the storms. On the outside of this glass work is a veranda made of iron, so that you may walk outside the glass. The view all around is sublime, extensive, and diversified. You may see Foula and the Fair Isle very well, Brassa, and to Lerwick, and the sea three parts round to the horizon. The lighthouse contains twenty-six reflectors which are concave, and copper finely plated with silver, and very bright; the manager stated they cost £50. each. It is a stationary light, to distinguish it from the revolving one on the Start point, in the Island of Sandy, in the Orkneys. At a distance the light house has a fine effect. The round tower and wings give it rather an oriental aspect. The road down from the light house winds about with a gradual descent North, until the ground becomes level with the sea. There is a good road made from the store houses by the sea side up to the lighthouse, to cart up the oil to supply the lamps, and other stores. There is a good farm and some tolerable grazing land below the head, occupied by Mr. Strong, the tax-man, and a few cottages. About a mile and a half north west of the lighthouse, are the ruins of the Jarls houses. Jarl is the manner in which the people pronounce 'Earl,' so that jarlshoos signifies the ruins of Earl Robert Stewarts house, and the ruins of the mansion of the former Lairds of Sumburgh. The remains of these ancient seats of revelry and grandeur, are dark, massive, formless ruins; the walls are more than a yard thick, and the windows small. The first story is nearly buried in rubbish, over which, and even on the walls, a rank grass grows. The only form remaining is a long narrow court, in which the cattle shelter in storms. About a hundred yards from hence are the ruins of the mansion of the ancient Lairds, at the end of which there is a flat square, which appears to have been a garden as may be seen by the ruins of the walls. There we see the withering vanity of earthly pomp, and the desolating and destructive power of time.

The gloom and solemnity of the place are now increased, as they have made a burying place around the ruins, and here and there you tread on graves, some covered by rude and shapeless stones. A few yards distance is a small square, roughly walled in, which is the family tomb, or burying place of the Lairds of Sumburgh. So that the place that was, formerly, one of sumptuous festivity, and noisy revelry, is now the stillest and most solitary. Leaving Sumburgh head and passing to Fitfill, you pass over a tongue or narrow strip of sand, which small strip alone keeps it from being an Island, cut off from the Mainland, as the sea comes up very near it, both from east and west. This sand is nearly a mile long, and was once green sward, but the surface was broken, then torn up and the light earth blown away, in some places from twelve to twenty feet deep; here and there small pieces still continue like pillars, covered on the top with grass. This gives great unevenness to the surface, as in other places nothing is left to the naked rock. The general appearance is very forlorn and desolate. Enobie is left east of Virkie. There is a school house, four miles from the parish kirk. The Wesleyans have a society here, and there is preaching monthly, in the school house, and in Virkie. There are also an exchange house and shop for bartering. The road is very broken and difficult, until you come to the sands on Quendal Bay, which are fine and nearly a mile long; on which the surges break with noisy roar. A few hundred yards north of these sands, may be seen the ruins of the old parish kirk; which, on account of the deluge of sand, and the badness of its situation, was permitted to become a ruin, and a new one has been built in a much better situation. There are but few vestiges of it left, but in the burying ground there are several stones still standing, and parts of monuments on several of which the arms of persons of distinction are yet seen, although some of them are broken, and others half engulphed. Many of the bones lay strewed and bleaching upon the sand. I examined the skull of an infant, and several other bones. I felt, at first, disposed to take what I took to be a finger bone as a curiosity; but after thought would not let me break in upon the sacredness of the grave, or offer an insult to the dead. The land about it is good for nothing, being covered with sand or water. At the end of the sands stands the mansion of the Laird of Quendal;

L

it would be looked upon as a good farm house in England. Mr. Grierson has been many years in the East Indies. I found him hospitable, intelligent, and friendly. The towns under Fitfill are Garth and Park, and some other towns of considerable size and fertility. To mount the top of Fitfill is a laborious undertaking; it rises perpendicularly, on the west, eight hundred feet above the level of the sea; and is composed of mica, slate, and clay. It runs north-west about three miles, and then is abruptly and ruggedly broken. From the top of Fitfill there are extensive views. In passing on the west side of the land, the road leads through Hilwell: here is a large cluster of cottages; a school house also, in which, and in several of the cottages about Fitfill the Wesleyans preach. You pass on the west side of several fresh water lochs, one about two miles long, in which there are fine trout. You pass some fine green land and two groupes of cottages, Noss and Spriggie. In Spriggie lives the pious deacon, who regularly preaches in the Baptist chapel. I believe he has some allowance from a society in Scotland, and his members also do what they can for him; he, therefore, never goes to fishing, or indeed employs himself in anything but his small farm and preaching. Passing over some sands between the large fresh water loch and a fine spacious bay from the atlantic, there is a large burn, by which the loch empties itself into the sea, over which is laid a log of wreck timber as a bridge. An attempt was made to drain this large loch into the sea, but it was found there was not sufficient fall.

This brings you to the road that runs half way up a steep hill between Scosburgh and Kerwick, which leads east to the kirk and chapels, and west to Kerwick and Bigtown. On a burn a little east of Scosburgh are about a dozen small water mills, in which they grind their corn. They are the smallest, simplest, and least efficient, that can be conceived: they are about three feet high and six or seven wide. The stones are made of micacious guiess. The iron goes through the top stone and then has a fan wheel; against the flat pieces of wood, eight or ten inches long, the water forces and works round the stone, many of which are fed by the hand, and others from a straw cathie, as an hopper. Here the poor people, without expence, grind their corn. Each groupe of cottages has a mill, and sometimes there is a mill to a single house. When they have long wanted water, when it comes they grind in turns, day and night; generally two for company's sake at night. When there is a necessity they grind in a handmill called the kurn.

Passing along the hill side to Kerwick, which in some places is precipitous and dangerous, should should the moon just rise over the lonely Fitfill, as it did when I first passed this way, the islets, mountains, and cliffs, interspersed with lochs, and the arms of the atlantic, the vast, deep shadows, the trembling reflections of the moon's beams, and the silence occasionally interrupted by the distant and softened roarings of the sea, is as sublime and solemn as anything in nature.

Kerwick consists of five or six cottages and a blacksmith's shop, with some good land for corn and potatoes, but uninclosed.

The blacksmith, James Brown, is the leader of the small Wesleyan society in the place, and in his cottage there is monthly preaching. He is an upright man.

From Kerwick to Bigtown is a mile on the west shore, which appears as if it had been broken by some violent eruption. Some of the holmns and skerries seem shaped so as to correspond with the Island from which they are only a few yards separated.

Near Bigtown is Saint Ranen or Ninian's Isle, though properly it is not an Island, as you may generally walk to it over the sand. It is nearly a mile long, and excellent grazing land. What makes it remarkable is, that on this small Island there was, formerly, a Romish church, from which the Island takes its name. But there is scarcely a vestige of it left, only the burial ground.

In Bigtown there are a few cottages, and the mansion of the Laird of Bigtown, who is the eldest son of the Laird of *Simbister*. He has lately enlarged the house and premises, and made many improvements on the estate. He is an advocate and magistrate. Mrs. Bruce is a pious lady, and very much inclined to the Wesleyans. Mr. Bruce is not at all bigoted; he has always been friendly and hospitable to the ministers of that denomination, and they frequently preach in his kitchen or outhouses, There is a Wesleyan society here which is visited monthly. North-west of Bigtown, are Ireland and Maywick, two small places close to the sea side. From Maywick sands you may take a boat to Avery and Burra, and up Cliff Sound to Scalloway; but it is frequently impossible to get a boat off on account of the heavy surge which rolls on the sand here. Over the hill east is Shannawick, and over the cliffs Conings-burgh, from whence I have taken you east, and come round to the same point by the west.

A tour from Lerwick to Scalloway, which is between four and five miles west.—The nearest way, and that generally tra-velled by persons on foot, is very desolate and lonely, for there is not a cottage, or a foot of cultivated land, from the sound of Lerwick to the vale of Tingwall. You leave the Dunrossness road at a small bridge above Upper Sound, and pass over some boggy ground near a number of peat pits; and, in a few hun-dred yards, you pass a loch and ascend the stony, and steep hill of Wick, at the top of which east, you see the fertile vale of Gulberwick, and the north sea; west, a hill rises, and in the other direction hills rise, one above another, in all their dark and naked sterility. In the first valley there is a burn which runs near some pits, and very boggy ground, so that you will generally have to take a very circuitous route to keep from sinking into bogs.

From the top of the next hill the prospect is increasingly dreary. The hills are not remarkably lofty, but the ground on the top of some of them is very cracked and broken. Where this is the case among the loose and decayed peat there is not a blade of vegetation. But on the more elevated parts, there is a kind of white, woolly moss, grows mixed with a little coarse, wild grass; and the sides of the hills are covered with heather. In the next valley a burn winds its lazy, dark stream (for the water is deeply tinged with brown from passing through the peat) round the foot of the hills, over a very irregular channel full of large stones. In this valley there are a great many peat pits, broken ground, and bogs, which make the road very difficult, and lead you to wind about in various directions, and frequently, to be leaping and jumping.

But though the land is so sterile and uncultivated for so many miles, these wilds, or scathold, as they are called, are very useful; for the cottagers can freely keep sheep, cows, and ponies upon it. The wild grass and heather land, for a great part of the year, afford tolerable food; and, in severe winters, the cattle near the sea side will come down from the hills, and sustain famishing nature upon the sea weed thrown up by the tides.

From the top of the hill, about a mile from Scalloway, you have a fine view of the town, the harbour, and the Islands in the atlantic as far as Foula. This ancient capital of the Islands is beautifully situated at the western extremity of a fertile valley, between two bold and sterile hills. The town is built around the harbour, and consists of a few score poor houses, and a few hundred inhabitants. But there are a good number of inhabitants in several groupes of cottages at a short distance, and in the Isle of Trondra, on the opposite side of the harbour. There are a few good houses; the house of Mr. Scott, the Laird of Scalloway, and another, in which the young Laird used to live. Mr. Hay, merchant of Lerwick, has a good house and shop, with which are connected extensive premises for coopers and other workmen; and warehouses connected with the herring fishery. There are two new houses built, I believe, by one of Mr. Hay's foremen. There are two houses where you may get some refreshment and a bed. They may be called public houses or inns, Mr. Irvine's and Williamson's. The harbour has a small pier for large vessels to come up to, and a small one for boats, on which stands a colossean wooden figure of Columbus, which belonged to a vessel of that name wrecked off here. The castle is one of the most attractive pieces of antiquity in Shetland; it is a square, massive, building, the outer walls and turrets of which are still standing.

It stands on a little elevation near the harbour, and is built of lime stone, which abounds in this neighbourhood; but the window and door sills, and ornamental work, are of free stone. This castle was built by Earl Patrick Stewart, in 1600, who seems to have had a taste for, or vanity in, building castles and palaces : he built the palace in Kirkwall about the same time. There is an inscription over the door which is now much defaced, but which I copy from Brand.

Patricus Orchadiœ et Zetlandiœ comes cujus fundamen saxum est domus illa manebit habilise contra si sit arena perit.

Which is—" Patrick Earl of Orkney and Shetland.

  That house whose foundation is on a rock

  Shall stand, but if on the sand it shall fall."

This was composed by the minister of North Mevan, a Mr. Pitcairn, at the request of the Earl; or rather, taken from the Latin Testament, Luke vi. 48. It is supposed the minister hereby intended to reprove his oppressions, and insinuating the house could not stand long that was built on so bad a foundation. The earl approved of the verse saying, " My Father built his house at Sumburgh upon the sand, and it has given way already ; but this of mine I have built upon the rocks, and it shall endure." But this was not the case, for after he was beheaded the house was not taken care of, and soon became a ruin. This ancient seat of grandeur is now desolate and forsaken. The huge tower remains, but all the interior is dilapidated, its chambers are filled with broken fragments and sand, and its rifted walls and dismantled battlements give unrestrained access to the roaring sea blast.

As Scalloway is the second town, and most important harbour in Shetland, except Lerwick, and as it is on the west side, and Lerwick on the east, it is a pity that goods could not be conveyed over land from Scalloway to Lerwick, or from Lerwick to Scalloway ; as by sea, from one harbour to the other, is upwards of sixty miles.

They have now commenced making a regular road between the two places for horses and carts ; but it proceeds slowly as each cottager has to pay so many days work towards it yearly ; and the people, generally, cannot be brought to see the utility of roads, and therefore they contribute their labour grudgingly

There is a road now that horses and carts too may travel upon between the two places; but the hills are so steep, the road so bad, and the distance increased several miles, that a new road is greatly needed.

There is no church in Scalloway: but the inhabitants attend the parish church at Tingwall, which is about two miles distant. The Wesleyans have no chapel here: but they have a small society, and monthly preachings in a small school house, to very crowded congregations, so that a chapel here is much needed.

The inhabitants of Walls, and of that part, frequently come from Vaila Sound to Scalloway in boats, round the headlands, when the weather is fine, and then they walk over to Lerwick. The most commodious way to Walls from Lerwick is, to ride a pony to Scalloway round by Tingwall, and then take a six oar'd boat to Vaila, or, if the sea be rough to Rawick, and from thence walk over a piece of bad ground east of Skeild, and make for Ogenness, and take a boat to Watsness, which is across a voe about two miles wide, and you are then only about a mile from the kirk and Bay Hall.

A tour to Walls over land, which is twenty-four miles north-west from Lerwick.—Leaving Lerwick you turn off below Mr. Hay's farm, on the same side before you come to Cleckern Inn, and pass between the two lochs, and ascend stony hill. When you gain the summit, if you turn round and look south, the sound is seen to great advantage; and the loch, in which are the ruins of the Picts castle. Beyond, jutting into the sea, is the Isle of Mousa; and, on a fine day, you may see Sumburgh head. East, over Mr. Hay's green fields, you have a fine view of part of Lerwick, called the " Hill Head," and over it in the distance Brassa and Noss. The road runs through a piece of very stony and barren land, and north-west you see nothing of cultivation. East as you descend a hill, there is an opening, and you have a fine view of Grimester and the rocks in the north mouth of the harbour, and Whalsey, and the Skerries. But, for several miles after, the prospect is confined by hills until you come to a groupe of cottages called Dean, when the prospect up the valley west, is more open, but at the end of the valley are dark, heathery hills. A fine clear burn winds its course from west to east over its pebbly bed, and empties itself into the voe, east. The sea here runs inland about two miles, close to the road. At the top of the voe, in the sea, is a black rock, called 'House Stack,' as it rises something in the shape of a house; and a little north of this you see the south end of the Isle of Glitness, a large grazing Island. This valley is tolerably fertile; the road ascends a fine hill, part corn and part grass land, to Windygrind, a gate placed in a sod wall. From the top of this hill you have an extensive view of the fertile vale of Ting-wall. This is considered the best land, and in the best state of cultivation, of any in Shetland. To the west you see the parish kirk, and the manse of the minister, Mr. Turnbull, and a few cottages and small farm houses are scattered through the valley. You also see, west of the kirk, the loch and holmn where was the ancient 'Law ting,' or court of the Foudrie. To the east is Laxfirth, where Mr. Hay has a country house. He has a bailiff, from Berwick, who has delved and drained thirty or forty acres of land, and walled it in, so that it is in a fine state of cultivation. I examined some land which had been manured with the entrails of fish, and the crops were excellent.

This valley extends from Laxfirth on the east to Scalloway on the west, and though not more than about four miles long, is the whole breadth of the Mainland. Beyond this valley you mount the rough stony hill of Whiteness, which is interspersed with several large bogs, into which the ponies frequently get, and out of which they dexterously struggle. From the top of this hill you have an extensive view of the west coast, which is rugged and broken, and near the shore are a number of small Islands and Skerries, with pieces of land running in curious forms out into the sea, over many of which the surges break and foam, and against others they dash and break in fury. At the bottom of this hill you cross a burn and find a few cottages. The track runs nearly at the bottom of a lofty hill very rocky heaving up for many feet, by places, perpendicular; it is com-posed of guiess. After passing round this hill, the first houses in Whitness and the school house appear. In this parish there was an ancient church called St. Olla's chair. Passing from the school house to Captain Cragie's house, you get a glance of Whitness kirk, which stands by the side of a fresh water loch several miles long. In the midst of this loch there is a small holmn, on which are some ruins where, it is said, a profligate son of one of the Earls of Orkney fled, from the displeasure of his father, and built himself a strong house in this holmn within the loch of Storm. His father sent from Orkney four or five men to pursue him, who were to bring him back dead or alive. The son, finding this house not sufficiently strong, fled and was pursued by these men who lay in ambush, and was overtaken in the Strath of Tingwall, between Tingwall and Scalloway, where there is an obelisk, or high standing stone, which marks the spot where he was slain. But it is questioned whether this stone does not mark the site of a bloody battle between the Norwegians and Picts, in which the Norwegian General fell. On the north-west side of this loch are several towns as they here call them; Strom, Quiness, and Stromford. This loch empties itself a little north of the school house into Eustaness voe, over the outlet of which a rude stone bridge is built. After passing Captain Cragie's and a few cottages near his house, you cross a swampy valley, and come to the foot of the hill of Benyness, along the side of which you proceed, and passing the airs of Strom and a few cottages, you shortly come to Weesdale sound, over which you are taken in a ferry boat for a penny; it is only a few hundred yards wide. Where you get out of the boat there are a few cottages, and a genteel looking house which is a kind of public house, where a Mr. Ross sells whiskey, and home brewed ale, and many other things. In the front of the house there are several trees planted, which have grown many feet high; this is a rare sight in Shetland. To the north-east up the valley are the town and parish of Weesdale, in which there is a school house but no kirk. The Wesleyans here are not permitted to preach in the school house, but they have a society, and preach monthly in a cottage.

M

South-west of Mr. Ross's is the remaining part of Weesdale parish, called Weesdale sound. Near Mr. Ross's house formerly stood a church, called 'our lady's kirk,' which was a favourite resort of superstition for a century after the abdication of popery. On these visits they would drop coins into the chinks of the ruins, and creep round on their bare knees. In removing some of the ruins a great quantity of coins were found, from the gilder down to the stiver. The parishes of Tingwall, Whitness, and Weesdale, form but one ministry, which formerly formed an archdeaconry; but a missionary, from the church of Scotland, has been appointed to assist this minister. Leaving Mr. Ross's, which is about ten miles from Lerwick, you ascend a steep hill, from the top of which the view is of amazing extent and grandeur; descending this hill the ground is very boggy; some of the bogs are sufficient to swallow a coach and six. At the bottom of the hill is Trestra, a few cottages on the side of *Bixetter* voe, which is an arm of the atlantic, and runs inland seven or eight miles. On the north west of Bixetter voe is a range of lofty barren hills. On the opposite side of the voe is the kirk of Simbuster in Sandsting parish. Those who walk generally prefer what is termed the ferry way, and cross in a boat from Trestra to Sandsting, near to Sand, which lies near the shore of the atlantic. There is a considerable number of inhabitants and cottages in Sand, and close on the sands of a large bay stand the Wesleyan and Independent chapels. They have a lonely and missionary aspect. In Sand is the delapidated mansion of Sir Andrew Mitchell, who died without any male issue. Many rooms of the house are yet let out to poor people.

After crossing a lofty, trackless, hill, you come to Sellivoe, at the head of which voe stands the manse of Mr. Bradon, the minister of Sandsting and Aithsting parishes. It is a neat sequestered spot. I observed all the windows in front had shutters, which are closed up in storms to preserve the glass in the windows. The hills beyond Sellivoe to Sellavoe are very high, and the face of the country wild, dreary, and trackless. You cross Sellavoe in a boat; on the opposite side you find some green grass land, and some corn land and houses. Here Mr. Henry keeps a shop and sells a little whiskey, it is a sort of public house. From hence to Grutting is about a mile. This is the place where John Nicholson lived, the old pensioner, who introduced Methodism into Shetland. The first class was formed at Grutting, of which he was the leader. From hence he went forth in his simple way, teaching salvation by believing, and a present and conscious salvation from the guilt and power of sin. Grutting consists of a few cottages which stand on the top of a hill, which is not generally the case on account of the exposure of such cottages to the storms. A short distance from the cottages is a small inclosed burying ground. Here John rests in his lowly bed, who laboured hard as a local preacher, to spread experimental and vital religion. When I mentioned something concerning him in the village, his name was as ointment poured forth, and several wept much while I conversed with them about his death.

At the foot of this hill is Grutting voe. In this neighbourhood there are the remains of several Romish chapels, Pictish castles, and concentric circles of stones. Grutting voe is said to be six miles deep, and yet is only one and a half wide. The rocks on the coast of Sandsting are rugged and precipitous, and are composed chiefly of granite, gueiss, mica, slate, and lime stone. From Grutting voe to Bay hall, to the Wesleyan chapel and parish kirk, is about an hours walk. But this ferry road, though preferable for persons on foot, is not so convenient for those who ride. The riding road is on the Aithsting side of Bixetter voe. You pass the Aithsting kirk, which is an old mean building, in the town of Twatt, near which are the house and chapel of Mr. Tullock, a lay preacher of the Independent denomination. You pass the head of Bixetter voe to Affirth, and then ascending a hill to the west, you pass the small town of Hockland. Troland is left to the east. This is a complete desert. You keep a south-west direction until you come to Stony Dale, where there is a small groupe of houses, and shortly you pass a bridge at the head of the voe of Brucland, and from thence to Brewster. You now enter the parish of Walls. To the west lies Stony Twatt: but in a direct line to Bay hall you pass a few cottages called Stove, where there is a respectable shop. From hence you see Vaila Sound, Bay hall the residence of the Wesleyan minister, and the kirk at a short distance. Around the kirk, and about the head of the sound, are several small towns, and the Methodist chapel which will hold nearly three hundred people. The scenery about Walls is rather confined as it is surrounded by bold and barren hills: but in summer it is remarkably interesting and romantic.

A Tour from Lerwick to North Roe, which is about Thirty-five miles north, in the Parish of North Maven.—The way to North Roe branches off east from the Walls road at Tingwall, and for a few miles there is a good road, until you pass Mr. Hay's farm at South Laxfrith, about which there are several interesting towns. The road goes about half a mile beyond Laxfrith, near to the east shore. The Isle of Glitness is opposite the end of the frith, and but a short distance from the mainland, with several small Islands about it, of very unequal and varying heights. The road ends as you enter a valley about a mile and a half long, with high hills on either hand, covered with heather, and before you four ranges, one beyond another, of dark hills, the highest and most remote of which is the east Karine. The ground is uneven and boggy, with peat pits in various directions; but on the foot of the west hill, at the end of a loch, there is some cultivated land and two cottages called Zoar; and on the east shore, on the side of Shalderness voe, is an interesting town, walled in, and the cottages of the best kind, called Wadbester.

A little beyond this, on rising ground north of Shalderness voe, is the green, pretty, little town of Girlstie; around which there are hundreds of acres of land, I may say, just as the deluge left it, which does not profit its proprietor a shilling an acre. There are the remains of several Picts houses about Girlstie, the rooms of which are under ground. North of Girlstie there is a beautiful fresh water loch, about a mile and a half long, with a small holm in it, in which the wild fowl nestle. The way from Girlstie to Catfrith on either side the loch is bad, and the ground is broken into deep and wide burns, and interspersed with many bogs, and peat pits. This is a bad piece of ground to travel over in winter. About half way up the west hill is Britoe, and over the hill east is Brunt Hammersly. Catfrith lies at the bottom of this hill, in a flat surrounded by hills. There are about a dozen cottages, and a tall white aule house which is occupied by Mr. Angus, who is a taxman and shopkeeper, and sells whiskey. This house was built for a linen manufactory but did not answer. There is in this flat a groupe of houses called Crown, or at least, on the side of the hill west.

From the top of Catfrith the land runs out many miles east, to Brough, which includes several small towns, Houland, Vassa, Haswick, and Eastwick, in most of which the Wesleyans preach and have societies. It was in this part of Nesting, called Garth, that the parish kirk formerly stood; the ruins and burial ground of which still remain. The present kirk is at Neap, which is much more central with the other two kirks belonging to this ministry, the one at Luna, and the other in the Isle of Whalsey. There were in Brough, a short time since, the remains of a dilapidated old mansion, formerly the seat of an old Baronet named Sinclair, or St. Clare, who was styled the Baron of Brough. This old mansion was pulled down just before I left the Island.

From Catfrith to Grubsness is over the Kaims, these lofty ranges of hills called the east, west, and mid Kaim. The valleys between these hills may be considered as vast bogs. From the tops of these hills you may see, on one hand, the atlantic rolling its deep blue waves to the horizon, and on the other the north sea mingling in indistinctness with the sky; the coast intersected by voes and bays, as though the sea and land with outstretched arms, embraced each other; and at a short distance from the shore, a number of Islands and holms, of various sizes and distances. The land has an exceeding wildness of appearance, without cultivation, without enclosures, without roads, nor even a cottage to be seen here and there; a loch reflected the double depth of the hills and skies. From the top of the last Kaim Olnafrith voe appears in sight, on the side of which stand a few cottages called Goudala, Grubsness, &c. There is one aule house occupied by Mr. Cooper, a fishery officer, in whose house the Wesleyan minister from North Maven preaches monthly. This is about half between Lerwick and North Roe. From hence to North Roe you take a boat across Olnafrith voe to Wathersta, which consists of some small pieces of cultivated land, a few cottages, and an aule house belonging to a factor of Mr. A. Gifford, Laird of Busta. It is said Lord Robert Stewart resided in Wathersta before he built his house at Sumburgh. On the other side of a voe from Wathersta, is the Seat of the Laird of Busta, which I shall shortly describe. At Brae, a little beyond Wathersta, the land becomes very narrow, as a long voe from the atlantic, out of St. Magnus Bay, runs inland past Busta up to Brae: and another voe from the north sea, out of Yell Sound. At the top of each of these voes, as you look towards the sea, are several small Islands. But narrow as the Mainland becomes here, it is much narrower about two miles beyond, at a place called Mavis Grind. Here the atlantic on the west, and the north sea on the east, have so nearly cut in two the Mainland, that North Maven would have been an Island, only for a few yards; over which narrow pass you may draw a boat out of one sea into the other. The poet has well described the tranquillity and solitariness of the place.

> " There, bosomed in a deep recess,
> Sleeps a dim vale of loneliness ;
> The circling hills all bleak and wild,
> Are o'er its slumbers darkly piled :
> Save on the sides, where far below,
> The everlasting waters flow ;
> And distant precipices vast
> Dance to the music of the blast."

Mavis Grind signifies the gate or entrance into the North Maven parish. Beyond this narrow pass the Mainland again assumes its usual breadth. After you have passed this a short distance, you travel along a valley, with lofty hills east and west, and for miles there is neither cultivation nor inhabitants. God has indeed spread upon it the line of confusion, and the stones of emptiness. As you approach the neighbourhood of Innisfirth, there are some neat cottages and some good land. Innisfirth excels any part of Shetland for scenery: here you have a union of the wild and tranquil, the mean and magnificent, the fertile and the sterile. The Wesleyan ministers visit this place from North Roe. The cottage where I stopped was placed at the foot of a rugged rock which rose perpendicularly, several hundred feet above it, with large overhanging masses, which, were they to fall, would crush the cottage and its inhabitants to pieces. A voe, from the atlantic, about a mile long, rolls up to the door, at the head of which are the boats drawn out upon land when they return from fishing.

From hence to North Roe is about seven or eight miles. The first part of the way the scenery is confined, and the travelling bad, constant leaping and jumping. To Colefirth the way for a great part is up valleys, till you come nearly to the foot of Rona, a noble, smooth hill or mountain, the highest hill in Shetland. A voe from the atlantic sweeps around a great part of his base. The Mainland here again becomes narrow, as the north sea at loch end has made an opposite approach. It is said that several alpine plants are found on the top of Rona. The head is frequently circled with clouds, so that the inhabitants on a clear day will say " Rona has got his cap off to day."

Colefirth, is a small groupe of cottages, from which you have a view of Loch end, on the other side of the voe west, in which stands an aule house, in part of which the Wesleyan minister used to live; but now there is a house built close to the chapel in North Roe.

The valley between Loch end and North Roe is, I think, as desolate and boggy as any you pass; but you are shortly gladdened by a sight of Yell Sound, and the houses scattered around the bay. At the end of the Mainland are the Wesleyan chapel and ministers house, which form one long low building. The house is but small; it was built only for a single man: it is a great pity it was not built rather larger so as to accommodate a married man, as the situation is so lonely for a single person. The chapel will hold between two and three hundred hearers, and is generally well attended, as it is eight or nine miles from the parish kirk. The chapel is built within a few yards from the shore, and the sea forms a fine bay in front, around which are a number of decent looking houses and a few good cottages; but the congregation comes for miles round. Yell Sound, which is in front of the chapel, is about eight or nine miles across. On a fine day you can see the houses in the Island of Yell, especially the beautiful white mansion of Mr. John Ogilvey, of west Sandwick. The scenery about here is very romantic. Jamison, in his Geological work, has well described the west parts of North Maven. "Many of the scenes, says he, are as wild and sterile as can well be conceived; grey rocks rising from the midst of marshes and lochs; shores bounded by awful sea beat precipices; do not fail to raise in the mind ideas of desolation and danger. The coasts in general are rugged, and precipitous, presenting in many places scenes truly grand and magnificent."

There are vast rocks of various heights a distance from the shore, dreadfully rugged and broken, opposing their rude fronts to all the fury of a tempestuous ocean, which in some places has formed great detached pillars, and in others excavated grand natural arches and caverns that mock all human magnificence, and strike the beholder with awe and wonder, which must affect every one on viewing these amazing wrecks of nature.

A visit to Rona's Hill principally by water.—I took a boat to Catfrith, which is about nine miles on the east side of the Mainland. As we passed up the harbour of Brassa Sound, I remarked that from the south to the north entry of the harbour is upwards of four miles. The south entry is at the Knab, and the north at Rovers Head. It is about a mile across from the Mainland to Brassa. The anchorage is from eight to twelve fathoms. There are several holms at the north end and about the north entrance of the harbour; the holm of

Craster, and two green holms. There are three sunken rocks in the harbour, and some in the north entry. The only remarkable one lies several miles out of the harbour, south by east of the Isle of Glitness, called the *Unicorn*, because on it the Unicorn was wrecked, when Kirkaldy was pursuing Earl Bothwell in his flight, of whose vessel they had sight, and who ran near the rock to mislead Kirkaldy who had no pilot; so that, following Bothwell's track, he was wrecked. In going to Catfrith you do not go out to sea, but keep near the shore, keeping west of the House Stack, the Brothers, and the Isle of Glitness, and a narrow strip of the Mainland, a part of Nesting, so that it is up a voe or arm of the sea.

You pass the end of Deals voe, Laxfrith voe, and Shalderness voe, which runs inland west out of Catfrith voe, which runs north. The rock scenery has nothing very bold or curious. Leaving the boat, Buchan Irvine, who accompanied me as my guide and companion, thought it advisable that we should take a little refreshment at Mr. Angus' before we mounted the Kaime. We got a bottle of porter and some ship biscuit. Mr. and Mrs. Angus are very kind and hospitable to ministers, in their journeying through the Islands. You only cross the East Kaime to Olnafrith voe, at the head of which the town of Voe is situated. The East Kaime is full of deep cracks, covered with heather, in some places with rank grass, and a white woolly moss. The prospect is much the same as before mentioned; I think, if any thing, more extensive, for you may see north to Rona, and to the north Isles, and south to Fitfill Head. Descending from the hill you come down into the valley near a loch. There is a burn which runs along the valley, on the sides of which there is a green pasturage, on which a few sheep graze. This burn divides the parishes of Lunisting and Nesting from Delting. At a short distance from the end of this valley is the town of Voe, consisting of about thirty-two cottages, and the aule house of Dr. Adie, a medical man, who was many years a surgeon in the East India service. He has two sons grown up, who live on the premises and keep a shop, and do something in the herring fishing. In Voe is a kirk belonging to the ministry of

N

Delting, in which they have a sermon every other Sunday. This town is called Voe, I suppose, on account of its situation at the head of this fine voe, which runs inland from the atlantic, in a winding direction, six or seven miles. I found several hills about Voe in a state of cultivation, which is not common.

We took a boat to Busta which is about nine miles from Voe. I called upon the Laird, Arthur Gifford, Esq. I had never seen him before, but he received me very courteously; and though they had dined, they soon placed a warm dinner before me, and both porter and wine. They would not hear of my proceeding any further that night, but promised to send me, early in the morning, by boat the nearest way, and that their men should stay and bring me back again to Busta. During the afternoon the Laird gave me an account of a very dangerous passage which he had to the south, (*i.e.*) Scotland, a few months before: he was out at sea, in a most violent storm, sixteen or seventeen days, in the Norna to Peterhead; his descriptions were vivid and affecting. He is a man of talent and education, and of very gentlemanly manners.

We took tea in the saloon, a long, ancient room, hung round with the family portraits of many past generations, and coming down to the present Laird and Lairdess.

Our party consisted of Mr. and Mrs. Gifford, and a neice, a Miss Hay from America, Mrs. Langridge, sister to the Laird, and a neighbouring gentleman. After tea Miss Hay played several pieces on the piano forte, with considerable execution.

Mr. Gifford has no children; Mrs. Gifford is sister to Mr. William Hay, merchant and banker, Lerwick.

A law suit has lately been decided in referenee to the Busta estate. The descendants of a second branch of the family wished to wrest it from the present Laird, but failed. The account of the trial I saw in print, which from memory I will briefly give. The family of the grandfather of the present Laird consisted of three sons, who in crossing from Wathersta to Busta, in a boat along with a young clergyman, some words passed which led to a quarrel; the boat was upset and they all perished. Great search was made for their bodies, but only the body of the eldest son was found; and while it lay upon the beach, in front of Busta, a Miss Pitcairn, who was lady's maid to the Lairdess, in the presence of witnesses, declared he was her husband, by whom she was then pregnant; and putting her hand into his pocket she pulled out their marriage certificate. They were privately married, I believe, by the clergyman who was drowned along with them, and the marriage kept private for fear of the displeasure of the old Lairdess, who was exceedingly proud and imperious. But the old Laird and Lairdess, being bereft of all their children, when this child was born, they acknowledged it and educated him as the heir to the estate. This child was Gideon Gifford, the father of the present Laird. But the descendants of the brother of the old Laird wished to prove that this child was illegitimate, and to cut off the present family as not lawful descendants, and to claim the estate; but the verdict was in favour of the present family.

Busta is of Norse origin. *Bu* signifies a cow, and *star* or *ster*, a stall or standing for cows or bullocks; so that it was, anciently, a celebrated grazing pasture, which is very likely from its present appearance.

The hall is something after the old baronial style; the windows narrow and small, stone stairs, and a bell in the lobby. The arms are over the door; the crest is a stag's head; the motto is " spare naught." The gardens and walks are very beautiful for Shetland. In the garden in front of the house, there are embowered walks under stunted sicamore trees, mountain ash, and alder; and in the gardens there are numbers of gooseberry and currant trees. The gates, at the bottom of the front garden, open upon a small pier, which has steps down to the sea, so that boats may come up close to the pier. The voe in front was as smooth and unruffled as a loch, and reflected, as from a mirror, the buildings and hills around. The green fields and finely cultivated land around Busta, form a striking contrast with the scenery north about the wart hill, which consists of mountains, wild, and sterile. Early in the morning we started in a boat for Rona's hill, which is about twelve miles from Busta.

We soon left the voe and entered Roe sound, a narrow, shallow sound between Muckle Roe and the Mainland. At the entrance of the sound there is a small Skerry, on which are the ruins of an old brough. Large stones are placed between it and the Mainland, at a convenient distance, which form a causeway, at low water, to pass to and from the Mainland. This sound winds around the foot of the hills of the Mainland into St. Magnus bay. As we entered the atlantic I was struck with the vast extent of the bay. The Mainland is seen stretching, in a circle, many miles north-west, at the end of which you see the Isle of Stenness and the fishing stations; on the south-west it runs out into the sea, and forms the entrance of the bay at Sandness and Papa. From this distant view of Papa Stour, the Island appears flat, and the white house of Mr. Henderson is just seen. Bearing west, wrapt in neutral tint, are seen the spiring cliffs of Foula. The bay is about twelve miles across. The swell of the sea was very great, though the day was fine, which is not to be wondered at when we consider, that the whole weight of the atlantic rolls into this bay, unbroken by any land between this and America. The west part of the Mainland of North Maven, which was to the east of us, may be styled the finest rock scenery of any around the whole Mainland. It consists of bold, lofty, broken precipices, at the bottom of which are a number of vast broken masses and caverns, so that the sight of these devastations, and the noise of the surges breaking over them, with the booming of the swell in the caverns, fill the mind with sublime emotions. Out of a number of fantastically shaped pillars, rocks, &c., I shall only notice two. The rock called the Drongs, composed of red granite, cleft from the top nearly to the bottom in three places. One mass is large and broad, like the sail of a sloop, the highest at one point, and then gently sloping down. It is said that when it is seen obscurely in a fog, it gives an idea of a vast ship under sail. On the east side of Stenness is also a lofty rock, called Dorcholm, perforated by a magnificent arch about one hundred and fifty feet high, and several hundred feet wide. Leaving the bay we entered Hillswick voe, when the swell of the sea ceased. Hillswick stands a short distance from a sandy beach. It consists of cottages in various directions, the house of Mr. Thomas Gifford, a farm house or two, the kirk of the North Maven parish, and the ministers house.

Leaving the boat on the beach, we had to walk a mile across a tongue of land, until we came to the voe that winds round the base of Rona, and runs inland about three miles. After crossing this voe, we came to the foot of Rona's hill, and, as the boatmen had never been at the top of the hill, they offered to accompany us. Rona is one vast mass of very bright red granite. It does not look so high as it is represented to be, but this may arise from its not being spiral, or conical, but a vast round-backed hill, being near two miles in diameter at the summit. The height of it is very diversely stated; from upwards of three thousand feet to considerably under two thousand. I should think it is about two thousand feet above the level of the sea. We had to rest many times before we reached the top. There are many little rills of water running down the hill, which frequently afford a necessary refreshment. From the top, the day being clear, we saw the whole extent of the Mainland; Fitfill, wrapped in grey, closed the view, which is about fifty miles distant; and north, to Unst, Yell, Fetlar, and Foula, the Drongs, Ashenness, or Oceanness, the rock Osee, and the Villans of Ure, (a piece of green pasture land.) The Mainland appears from hence very broken and shattered. I saw the voes winding in various directions, and upwards of twenty lochs, and fifteen or sixteen towns. Some light clouds were rolling over the sea beneath us, and the gulls were sporting far below. The top was level and, generally, void of any vegetation; in some places as smooth as slab stones, and in others it is covered with small fragments of stone, as though macadamized. The air at the top was perceptibly keener.

I left Rona perfectly satisfied for the pains I had taken: we found our boat safe on the beach, and hastened back to Busta.

The wind springing up brisk towards evening, I got put on shore at Nebin, and we walked over land, hoping that the inland scenery on the west shore would amply repay us for the walk. We were forced to engage a woman, who lived near the shore, to guide us until we came within sight of Mangester, which is a beautifully sequestered spot. The scenery from here to Alesbrook, and from thence to Mavis Grind, is more lofty than the coast, and is of the wild, romantic, Matlock scenery. At the top of some of the highest hills there are large masses of grey rock, resembling fortresses, or the round towers of old castles. About eight o'clock, very weary, we arrived at Busta. The next morning Mr. Gifford accompanied us down to the pier, and saw the boat well ballasted, as he said, for want of this, many lives had been lost. We sailed to West Burrafirth, and passed through Weesdale again to Lerwick.

I will close my description of these Islands by briefly stating that they frequently present some of the grandest imagery referred to in the Sacred Scriptures, and by the most distinguished poets. The waves lifting up their voice; the surges rolling with resistless sweep; the dash and roar of many waters; the raging waves of the sea foaming out their shame; the foam of the rock-beating surf; the steadfast promontory on whose base, angry, tempests beat, while sunshine gently settles on its brow; the wild fowl gracefully dancing on its waves, and the frail skiff heaving on its bosom; the mists rolling up the sides of the mountains, at the approach of the orb of day; the wilderness and the solitary place, and the eagle, and the bittern, and the cormorant, are there; and, frequently, the eagle is seen soaring with no middle flight.

THE NATURAL HISTORY OF THE ISLANDS.

The geology of these Islands is so interesting, that Dr. Jamison and Dr. Hibertson visited them, for the purpose of geological investigation, which they have published. One of Dr. Hibertson's discoveries has proved a considerable source of wealth to several of the Lairds. I refer to his discovery of the *Cromate of Iron*. I believe there are some minerals there of excellent quality and great worth. I found an earth, in considerable quantities, nearly equal to Terra de Sennie; when ground, it was a transparent yellow; and when burnt, a transparent red, or deep mahogany tinge.

The specimens of primitive rock are numerous, and beautiful. The white, grey, and red granite, guiess, mica, slate, micacious spastus, hornblend, quartz, primitive lime stone, and serpentine; also curious specimens of transition and association rock.

Metals have been found, but to no extent; and a few gems; nodulus of chalcedony, porphyry, onyx, sardonyx, and some rare fossils. The animals in Shetland differ a little from both England and Scotland. There is no game in them, not even Moor game. They have a few rabbits and wild fowl. There are snipes, wild ducks and geese, wild pidgeons. The stormy patron is found here, and the great northern diver, the eider duck, Amber and Solon goose; and frequent flocks of wild swans, while passing over, settle upon our lochs; and eagles build on the bold promontories. The heron is here also, and the cormorant, and various gulls. There are no venomous creatures, toads, serpents, &c., not even frogs. The marine animals are seals, otters, porpoises, whales, sharks, sea dogs; fish are, cod-fish, ling, tusk, sellock, pellock, herrings, and turbots. The herring and mackerel are supposed to spawn and rest about the North Pole, so that vast shoals of them are, for some time, among these Islands, and in the sea at no great distance all around. The pises, or porpoises, are numerous in these seas; they are six or eight feet long; they have a singular method of rolling in the sea; their fat makes fine oil.

The cattle are small and suited to the Islands; the ponies are small, but lively, strong, and tractable. The dogs are of great use here in keeping the cattle off the cultivated land, and in catching sheep in the wilds.

PART THE THIRD.

THE MANNERS AND CUSTOMS OF THE INHABITANTS.

THERE is no middle class in Shetland, except a few shop-keepers in Lerwick, who have risen, generally, from the steadiest and most enterprising of the common sailors and fishermen. But in the country there are only the Laird and his tenantry or servants; for each Laird has several hundred persons who live on their estates, who are bound to serve them at certain times, "and they call them master and lord, for so they are., So that the distance between the poor and rich is a gulf that cannot be passed; there is, therefore, nothing to prompt emulation, or excite a desire to rise, there being no class a little above them to rise into; the cottages being all nearly the same; each one having about the same quantity of land, and pursuing the same occupation—that is, fishing.

A middle class is also of vast utility among any people, because they mingle with both classes, so as to receive and transmit, from the highest to the lowest class, sentiments and manners. Where this is the case, civilization is more rapid, general, and perfect. This middle class being wanting in these Islands, is the cause of more and greater evils than many suppose. They neither hope, nor endeavour, nor expect to rise above their present class, or their servile state; and as to the improvement of their habits of cleanliness, order, and domestic economy, &c, this can only be brought about by imparting intelligence, taste, manners, &c.; which needs higher intercourse, and greater means. It may, therefore, be said, "by whom shall Jacob rise for he is small." At the close of this paragraph I would briefly state my opinion—That nothing has done more, or is doing more, to make up the want of this middle class, than the itinerating of respectable ministers among them; for the expectation of their visit leads to the use of some efforts after more than ordinary cleanliness; and their living, and sleeping, and conversing, for ten or twelve days together, in various districts, has led to many improvements, The cottage where the minister goes monthly has procured plates, metal spoons, knives and forks, and a bed; things which were unknown until the minister visited them. The other cottagers, seeing their increasing comfort and respectability, imitate them, and hope occasionally to be the entertainer of the minister. This, and the spread of vital, experimental religion, will do much towards bettering the civil and social condition of the peasantry of Shetland.

The first class, or the gentry of Shetland, consists of the principal Lairds, opulent merchants, persons in offices under government, and a few professional men, who are principally of Scotch extraction, their progenitors coming from Scotland to purchase land of the Udallers; and most of the official situations are filled by persons from Scotland. They differ, therefore, but little from gentlemen in Scotland, most of them having finished their education in one of the colleges of Scotland, and many of them having travelled in various parts of the world.

They are conversable and polite, but their circumstances and situations have a strong tendency to make them proud and imperious.

They are much linked together by marrying and intermarrying, so that they form a strong confederation. They have, in winter, card parties very frequently, and, occasionally, balls and concerts; on which occasions, many of the established ministers consider it right to be present and take a part.

They appear less attached to the forms of religion than the common people, but yet many of them keep up appearances, although there are very few who may be denominated decidedly religious.

They are fond of politics, and the Lairds are generally WHIGS; many of the professional and official gentlemen are TORIES; and at the last election they manifested considerable party spirit.

They are very hospitable and kind to respectable strangers, and pay tribute to superior talents and learning. This was manifested in the uncommon kindness shown to Dr. Mc'Alum, Dr. Clarke, and the Rev. James Everett; the characters and talents of whom are still held in the highest admiration. But the most excellent and honourable trait in the character of the Shetland gentlemen is, their entire freedom from persecuting and intolerant principles. I know of no Laird who uses any constraint in religious matters, or lays any restraints on the consciences of his tenantry.

The country people, or peasantry, take in the whole population in all the Islands, out of Lerwick, except the Lairds, a very few taxmen, and two or three who may be termed farmers. In person they are not remarkable, being much of the same size and complexion as persons in Scotland; but the countenances of some are truly Scandinavian. But few of the country women are beautiful, their mode of living and labouring injures their health, shape, and complexion, many of them are of a very sallow complexion and haggard look. They dress, ordinarily, in *wadmall*, a coarse flannel of their own manufacturing. That which is next the skin is white, the petticoat red, and the jacket, or gown, blue. The men, generally, have a sailor's dress, except when they go to the fishing, when many have a sheep skin suit. Their common shoes, in which they travel, are called rivlings a kind of sandal, made of cow's, or seal's hide, dried. The flesh side is put to the foot, and the hair outside, they are drawn round the foot and tied above the ancles. But most of them have regular shoes for the Sabbath; on week days most of the young go without shoes and stockings. On the head they wear a knitted cap, but many, of late, have got a canvass hat painted black, which is most suited for the sea. On the week day many are half naked, but most of them are smart and clean on Sundays; they are rarely seen with bonnets, and many of the old women have a white or black handkerchief pinned about their head, to answer the double purpose of cap and bonnet.

The language originally spoken was the Norse, and which was spoken in Unst and Foula within a century; but now the

English language is spoken throughout the Islands; but it is corrupted with many Norse, Dutch, and Scotch words, and pronounced with a peculiar accent.

Their cottages are poor, low, mean places, a mere shed, built with loose stones, and sometimes part with sods, the interstices being afterwards stopped with lime or clay, but, frequently, with nothing. The inside is open to the ridge, without any thing but the ground for a floor, no fire place, chimney, or window. They have holes in the ridge to emit smoke and admit light; sometimes a pane of glass is placed in the roof. There is a division of the cottage by a small partition, or wall, one part is called *But*, and the other *Ben*, or *Buin*. The But end is where they live, the Ben where they sleep. They generally place in front of the Cottage the *Bier*, the place for the Cows, &c., so that you pass through a dark, long lobby, full of manure, before you arrive at the door entering the Cottage.

They are covered in with, first, thin sods called feils, and then, some straw is spread over the sods, which is bound down with straw ropes, called cimons, which are bound very close together, and tied at the bottom to heavy stones, which hang as weights to keep all firm. The roofs never overhang the walls, but drip upon the centre, which makes the walls, generally, damp. I cannot tell the reason for this, unless it be to save wood, or to make the roof as low as can be, that the winds may have less power upon it.

The cottages are nearly the same throughout all the islands. To the cottages, in general are attached from three to five merks of land; a merk is about an english acre and a half. This is held by a *feudal* tenure, in which, part of the rent is paid in *service*, or labour, and gifts to the Laird; and two or three pounds in money, or in fish to that amount. The Laird finds them boats, lines, &c. The fishing is divided into the grey and white fishing, or short and long line. The grey is caught with short lines near the shore; this is the Seeth, or Cole-fish. The white are caught with the long line, out at the deep sea, which are Ling, Cod, and Tusk. There are, generally, six men in a boat for the long line fishing, which, according to

Dr. Edmonstone, seldom realizes more than about 12£. a boat during the three months fishing; that is about 2£. a man. Others fish in small sloops, some of which go over to the Ferroe Islands and stay until they get full; but they have not answered well, though it is much safer for the men; for those who go to the haaf, in small boats from twelve to sixteen feet of keel, forty or fifty miles out at sea, are in great jeopardy and frequently perish. It was while prosecuting this haaf fishing, that the dreadful boat-wreck took place in June 1832. The Rev'd J. Knowles says, " On Sunday I preached to many for the last time. On Monday, the day being very fine, they spread their whole canvass to the wind, to hasten to the fishing ground. About four o'clock on Tuesday morning the wind rose, and increased until it blew a gale. On Tuesday the scene was moving in the extreme; the winds and waves raging, and many hearts fearing and failing; wives, mothers, daughters, sisters, were running in various directions, heedless of the storm, to look from the top of some hill or cliff, for the appearance of the frail bark which contained their nearest and dearest relatives. Some were in sullen stupor, others in frantic agony; but all seemed to breathe out a prayer for their safety or salvation. The storm continued to rage, with but little abatement, for four days. These were days of awful suspense and sorrow, for there were but few in the north isles who had not relatives contending with the storm, and for whose safety they felt trembling anxiety. But few ever returned, and about one hundred widows and orphans were left to lament their loss"

Hundreds every year go to the Straits and Greenland in the whalers. This the young men do as the most lucrative, (if they are successful) to enable them to raise a few bettermost clothes, and a little ready money, before they marry. The Herring fishing has also been much increased within these last few years. In 1834, I believe, Mr. Hay cured fifteen thousand barrels. This fishing is very beneficial, because it prolongs the time of labour, and may be prosecuted after the long line ceases. The first commences in May, and finishes in the end of July. Then the Herring fishing commences and continues to September. It also finds employment for women, girls, boys, and old, infirm, men.   But still fishing is very precarious, and as they sometimes say, " if the sea shuts its mouth who can open it."

The few merks of land they have is laboured by themselves, and cultivated entirely in reference to their own support.   In spring, before the fishing commences, they dig it ; this is called the *voir*.   They dig with spades about the width of the hand, of very singular form ; and they dig together, three or four in company, and all heave at one piece, but they do not lift nor turn over the clod.   They heave it from one side to the other, and then throw a little loose earth from the bottom over it, never turning the spade.   They carry the manure in straw baskets, called Kishey, on their backs, or on ponies, in these Kisheys ; this is generally the work of the women.   They, generally, grow on the land Oats, Bear, or Biggar, a coarse kind of Barley, Potatoes, and Cabbage ; which are, generally, when the year is favourable, sufficient to serve the family.   After the fishing is over, they commence their harvest, which they reap, and gather, and thrash, and grind, and eat.   They keep a cow or two upon the Scathold, tethered at a short distance, but after harvest they graze about the land.   The sheep also run wild on the hills.   In the latter end of May the sheep are gathered off the hills, and driven into a round fold, built of sods, which each town has appropriated to it.   Every one then owns his sheep, for they are marked on the ears : each family has its mark, which is registered in the parish book.   The family mark always goes to the youngest son, because they suppose before he is brought up the Father will be an invalid, or dead.   When the elder sons are grown up they must invent a new mark for themselves.   They cut it in paper, and have it entered as their mark in the parish book, for which they pay one shilling and four-pence.   The sheep are of various colours, brown, yellow, piebald and grey.   When they find one with their mark they pull the wool off with their hands, which is not difficult, as a coat grows under, and they would cast it in time.   The wool is very valuable to them.   They wash it, card and spin it, and then

part of it they knit into stockings and gloves ; the other part
is woven into cloth, called Wadmall, of which the common
garments of the men, women, and children, are made. The
stockings and gloves they barter with the Lerwick merchants,
for tea, sugar, tobacco, draperies, &c. They are exported, and
are much valued by many for the softness of the wool ; some of
the stockings and gloves are astonishingly fine.

They pay tiends for every cow, sheep, and sheaf of corn, and
for every six oared boat. They also pay Scat-duty, Umboth
duty, the hawk hen, and to the school-master. They have also,
in some places, to pay the Laird so much butter, oil, eggs,
fowls, and so many days work whenever he requires them.

Fishing and knitting are the only regular means of earning
money, except by a few employed in making kelp. But there are
others which may be considered precarious and occasional ;
God-sends, as the people call them ; namely, the driving on shore
of whales, and the salvage of wrecked goods which they preserve.

Whale catching is not a regular, but accidental, employment.
The whales which visit these shores are the Ca'ing, or bottle
nosed whale, which go in shoals. They are, generally, discovered by some of the fishing boats, and, as soon as discovered,
a signal is made, in order that the other boats may come and
assist in driving them into creeks, or voes, towards the shallow
water inland. The whales are exceedingly tame and timid, and
suffer themselves, generally, to be driven before the boats, like
a flock of sheep. Sometimes, when the foremost feel the bottom,
they begin to be restive, and turn about, and dive under the
boats, and endeavour to escape to sea again. The fishermen
then pursue and surround them, and endeavour to turn them
back by beating the water with their oars, throwing stones, and
making noises. It is often a work of danger, and a considerable
time before they can get them on shore ; and frequently, after
much time and toil, they lose them. Others I have known
that have run ashore of themselves ; which, it is thought, have
mistaken their way, or have been pursued by some ravenous
sea monster. When the whales get on shore, they so beat about
and blow, that their strength begins to fail, for the sand gets

into their gills; and then they rush forward with such force that they are nearly out of the water. Such as offer to escape, they meet and attack with old harpoons, or lances, or large fish knives, or indeed, with any thing which will cut and wound them. When wounded they rush forward with prodigious force, and carry with them a large body of water, which retires and often leaves them on the shore. When they drag them more on the beach, they thrust their hands into the hole through which they breathe and blow; but they are careful, above all things, not to touch their eyes, for this would make them exceedingly restless, and with a stroke of their tail they might do much injury, for they have amazing strength in their tail.

The sea, in consequence of the slaughter, becomes red as blood; and others, which have not been wounded, it is said, are blinded and bewildered; and if they escape, will return to the bloody water again, and in their turn fall a sacrifice.

On the 22nd of August 1834, I saw two hundred and eighty driven upon the sands of Voxter. The scene I shall not soon forget. There were about three hundred men drawn together. The whales were strewed on the beach. They are jet black, and as smooth and bright as a silk glazed hat. The blubber is on the outside, all round the body, which when flinched is about eight or ten inches thick, much resembling flitches of bacon. After the blubber is taken off, the flesh is as red as beef, and streaked with yellow fat; in fact I could not have told it from beef. They are, generally, from under twenty to above thirty feet long. I saw a young one, taken from one, six feet long. They have a pair of fins something like arms, smooth and something resembling the wing of a fowl when plucked. With this fin they hold the young to their breasts. I was told that out of the breast of one, when flinched, milk flowed. The head of one I saw, which was cut off, weighed three hundred pounds weight.

Out of the whales thus secured, I believe Lord Dundas, as having the crown rights, can claim a share for the *king* The english law claims fish royal; they are the whale and sturgeon, when they are either thrown on shore, or caught near the coast. But, I believe, this claim Lord Dundas has relinquished, or it is not usually made. The Laird, on whose shore they are driven, claims, I think, one half. But the english law does not allow this; it says, concerning the right and property of fish, " It has been held that where the Lord of the manor has the soil on both sides of the river, it is good evidence he has a right to the fish; but where the river ebbs and flows, and is an arm of the sea, there it is common to all; and if the Laird claims any share, merely on account of their being driven on shore in his land, the *onus* falls upon him to prove his right. But if the right arises from any feudal right or agreement, that is a different matter, and the tenants ought to know of such agreement." There is but a small allowance, to each man, of a few shillings. The Laird, frequently, has four or five hundred pounds.

The vessels wrecked on these shores were, formerly, very numerous. But since the light house has been built on Sumburgh Head there have not been so many. It is said much inhumanity and injustice were formerly exhibited by the islanders, when ships were wrecked. But their conduct, in this respect, is improving; and, I believe, wrecked seamen never meet with more sympathy and kindness any where than in Shetland. For most of them having relatives at sea, and numbers having themselves been wrecked, there is a chord of sympathy touched on such occasions.

But I cannot say that they have as strict views of the immorality of keeping wrecked goods, as a custom house officer, or, I may say, as every true christian ought to have. *Flotson* signifies those goods which float on the sea when the ship is sunk; *Jetson* is a term referred to goods thrown overboard, to lighten the vessel, notwithstanding the ship is lost; *Lagan* signifies heavy goods cast into the sea, which sink, but a buoy is fastened to them, to tell the place where they are. " The King shall have" says english law " Flotson, Jetson, and Lagan. When the ship is lost , and the owners of goods are unknown, they are to be kept a year and a day, to give an opportunity for persons to make the claim." But a salvage is

P

paid, so much per cent, to the persons rescuing them from the deep.   There are, frequently, wrecked pieces of timber washed on or near the shore, which, if damaged, they keep; but, if perfect, they are given up to the custom house; these they may keep by paying the duty.   Wood being so valuable in Shetland, and money scarce, they are frequently tempted to find a flaw in the timber when there is none.

It is evident from these statements that they can earn but little money regularly.   Many with a wife and family, taking seven years together, will not earn above two or three pounds a year.   This goes to pay their rent, and the *wife's* knitting is bartered for a few luxuries, as " a corn of tea," for they seldom have any sugar.   Thus they literally live; many of them without money, and many have not a shilling in their possession for years.   Tea is a luxury but rarely enjoyed.   Their living consists of, in the morning, *thick porridge*, oatmeal boiled in an iron pot until it is thick.   This being poured into a large bowl, each being provided with a large horn spoon, they sit round, all eating out of the same vessel; to flavour which, they, generally, have a little curdled sour milk, but some prefer a little fresh milk.   The second meal is not, generally, until four or five o'clock, when they boil a pot full of potatoes and fish, which when the weather will permit, they have fresh every day; but if not, they have fish dried in the *air*, called *vivda*, which is of a sour tainted taste.   The potatoes and fish are then poured into a wooden trough, about two feet long, and about half that wide, which is placed on a stool.   They all sit round the trough. The women and children skin the potatoes with their fingers, and *eat with the same*; the men, frequently, have a pocket knife, called a *jockerleg*, with which they peel theirs, and eat their fish in their hand.   They eat nothing but unleavened bread, and their common beverage is *bland*, a sort of whey mixed with water and kept till it ferments and is sour.   They have seldom more than two meals a day.

The beds in which they sleep rather differ.   Some of them are one above another, in a corner, like large broad shelves. The first boards are placed near the floor, and then about two or three feet above, there is a second shelf. I have seen a third above that. On these boards they lay loose straw, or dried sea-weed, with a blanket over the straw, and a blanket and rug above it; so that in this small space a whole family will sleep. The children at the bottom, the master and mistress in the middle, and the old mother, or sisters, &c, at the top. But others, of the more respectable kind, stand on four feet, and are about two or three feet from the ground, and resemble a cupboard, and have a slide door.

Three or four of these will be placed on each side of *Ben* end, which only leaves a narrow space between them; but inside they are much the same as the others, only much warmer.

They seldom fully undress themselves, but only throw off the outer garments and loose the others.

They, formerly, had a very barbarous and bad custom, and even now it prevails to a lamentable extent, that is, of persons of all ages and sexes sleeping promiscuously together; a man and his wife, and children, and servant, or brother and sisters, &c.

After a young man contracts to marry a young woman, for several weeks before marriage they sleep together; but the custom is, that the sister of the intended bride sleeps with them.

Marriage is a private contract. The ceremony, which is very short, is always performed in private. The women wear no rings. They, generally, have a great party at weddings, and dance all night, and have a good deal of revelry. The sword dance, which is a relick of the ancient Norwegian customs, is frequently performed at country weddings.

It requires but very little to enable young persons to begin housekeeping; and they can make almost every thing among themselves. Most of them can joiner a little, and make themselves shoes, and tailor a little. In setting up housekeeping, there needs two or three home-made chairs; a small table, or high stool; a gridiron, on which they daily bake their bread, over a few glowing embers of peat; a colley, that is, an iron ancient looking lamp, as nothing is burnt but fish oil. A quern is in almost every cottage, that is, a hand-mill, in which they grind their daily bread, when there is no water to work the mill. The bags in which they put the meal are made of sheep skin; and a cupboard bed, or shelf for a bed. These few things attained, they are qualified to begin the world.

They marry young, and it is a rare thing to find a bachelor; and though they have so much privation and poverty, they appear to have much affection for each other, and enjoy much connubial hapiness, So that Solomon's proverb seems here verified, " A Dinner of herbs with love and peace is better than a stalled ox with strife.

They have no poor-laws, so that the poor are, frequently, very wretched. They have some small relief from the weekly offerings at the Kirk door, and the sacramental collections. They also go from house to house and stay a few days, or beg a little meal, or a bit of fish, or a few potatoes. In Lerwick the poor beg at each respectable house or shop weekly, or fortnightly, one half each. But in most cottages there is an old woman, the wife or husband's mother, for the children, generally, take care of their aged parents, and but few of them but can do something, bake the cakes, or knit, &c, which helps a little. The children soon become useful; for from some little skerry, or from a boat, with a little thread and a crooked pin, they can catch vast numbers of sillock, a small fry about the size of sprats; and piltock, the sillock a year older, which are about the size of mackerel and as fine eating; of the liver they make oil.

What seems very surprising to a stranger is, to find that nearly every poor cottager keeps a servant girl. It was surprising to me that they could get them; and, secondly, that they could support them. But they have, generally, plenty of fish and potatoes; and they will hire a maid for the winter four months for five shillings, and the regular wage is only a pound a year. The girl is needed to assist in digging the land, in carrying the peats from the hills, and in attending the cow or cows, sheep, and other things. In seed-time they drag the harrow after the seed, and in harvest reap, and dig potatoes, and grind, and thrash, and clean the corn, &c.

At the time of casting the peat, a man invites four or five of his relatives and friends to come and assist him in casting peat; and he makes a supper and gets a little ale or whiskey. This is the only remuneration they have; and in a day they will cut as many peats as will last them a year; and in return they assist others. This is the first work before *voir*, that is, the digging of the ground commences.

There is no market through the islands, which is a great disadvantage. Many things are bartered away in the country, or in the different islands; but most of the eatables are brought to sell in Lerwick, so that the supplies are very irregular and precarious, but very cheap. Potatoes are ninepence or tenpence a lispund, or anchor, which is thirty six pounds weight.

The weights and measures in the country are still Danish. They weigh by the bismer. The Danish and Dutch coins are still in extensive circulation. Eggs are three-halfpence and two-pence a dozen; Fowls ten-pence and one shilling a couple; a goose for one shilling or fifteen-pence; beef two-pence a pound, but you, generally, purchase a cow or bullock at once; mutton is frequently carried about the town at three-halfpence a pound, and pork under two-pence. But every thing which has to be imported must be expected a little higher, as wheat, flour, groceries, and draperies, &c.

The civil condition of the Shetlanders is a subject that has occasioned much litigation and strife. That their condition is bad, *is certain*, but it is difficult to say what is the cause. Whether it arises from the poorness of the land, the badness of the climate, the precariousness of their profession, the evils of the feudal tenure and want of larger portions of ground and leases, or a union of all these, is hard to ascertain.

Manufactures have been tried, and abandoned on account of the distance from the emporium. There wants more public spirit in the islands, to promote cultivation and manufactures, on the plan of Mr. Geo: Dempster, by which several of the Hebrides have been much improved. It is well known that the late Earl of Findlater, in the course of twenty or thirty years, introduced good agriculture and extensive manufactures into a part of the kingdom where neither were known before. Mr. Hay and Mr. Ogilvey employ a number of men in their merchandise and improvements.—might not others do the same?

SUPERSTITIONS.

Dr. Edmonstone says that the peasantry are very superstitious. They firmly believe in necromancy, and, I may say, also in witchcraft. But on no subject are they more superstitious than that which relates to fishing. Some of the more skilful prophets can foretel, from knots in the bottom boards of a boat, whether it will be lucky to fish or not; and whether it will be overset under sail, or be otherwise cast away; and boats have been rejected and torn up in consequence of such a prophecy.

When they go to fishing they carefully avoid meeting any person, unless it be one who has long enjoyed the reputation of being lucky.

Nor when the boat has been floated is it deemed safe to turn it but with the sun.

They also observe omens. When at sea they seldom call things by their usual names, but by Norwegian, for the Norwegians are reported to have been successful fishers.

Certain names must not be mentioned while setting their lines, especially the *minister* aud the *cat*.

There are also many wonderful accounts of singular appearances at sea.

Brand says, " About two years and a half or three years ago, there was a boat passing the Voe of Quarf, with several gentlemen of the country in it, when there appeared something unto hem with its head above the water, which, as they could discern, had a face of an old man with a loug beard hanging down. First it appeared at some distance from them, and then coming nearer to their boat, they had a clear sight of it. The sight was so very strange and affrighting, that all in the boat were very desirous to be on land.

I heard another remarkable story, — that, about five years since, a boat ut the fishing drew lines; and one of them, as the fishermen thought, had a great fish upon it, as it was with greater difficulty than the rest raised from the ground; but when raised, it came more easily to the surface of the water; upon which, a creature like a woman presented itself at the side of the boat. It had the face, arms, breasts, shoulders, &c, of a woman, and long hair hanging down to the back, but the other parts below the breasts were beneath the water. The fishermen being surprised and alarmed at this strange sight, one of them unadvisedly drew a knife and thrust it into her breast; whereupon she cried, as they judged, " alas," and the hook giving way, she fell backwards and was no more seen. The hook being large went in at her chin, and came out at the upper lip. The man who thrust the knife into her never prospered after it, but was haunted by an evil spirit in the form of an old man, who, as he thought, used to say to him " will you do such a thing who killed the woman "

There are also many accounts of sea monsters, mermen and mermaids, also sea frows, great rolling creatures tumbling in the waters; which, if they come among their nets, break them and sometimes take them away; and as they feel such a panic of fear, many of them think it is the devil assuming these shapes.

Witches and witchcraft are still believed in these Islands; and, even now, some old women live by pretending to be witches, as few dare to refuse them their requests. &c.

"About six years ago," says Dr. Edmonstone," a man entered a prosecution, in the sheriffs court at Lerwick, against a woman for witchraft. He stated that she uniformly assumed the form of a raven, and in that character killed his cattle and prevented the milk of his cows from yielding butter. The Sheriff expostulated with the man upon his folly and dismissed the case.

There is a domestic Trow, called Brownie, which is said to have been, formerly, so common that they attended on almost every family; and would, during the night, thrash, brew, churn, grind corn or malt, or sweep the house; but it was requisite that the persons made an offering for each night's work of a little wirt, or cream. &c. This would ensure good ale and butter, and preserve the stacks in a storm. &c. These Brownies, in catholic times, were said to be the souls of men who were doomed to wander and serve on earth until their crimes were expiated.

The reformed Divines did not deny their existence, but accused them of being fallen spirits in league with the devil, and exhorted them to resist the devil, and not to offer to them and they would flee from them. Brand gives an account of their mischievous tricks after they ceased to offer to them, but the but the visits of Brownie are now scarcely ever heard of.

But still the Trows and Fairies continue, are believed in, and frequently seen and contended with. It is believed the Trows steal away women and children, and substitute others in the place of them. This is the case when persons are taken speechless, or when any mental fatuity comes on individuals. No inducements can persuade some families, labouring under this impression, to afford to the sufferers proper care and attention.

On these melancholy occasions, persons are to be found who pretend to have the power of entering the caves of the Trows, and restoring them invisibly back to their friends; then they are immediately convalescent and of sound mind. An individual in Walls is said to have become rich by this profession.

Fairies hours are noon and midnight, when they dance or ride through the air on bulrushes. If persons meet them without a bible in their pocket, they save themselves by drawing a circle round themselves, and forbidding the Fairies to come nigh; though some persons profess to have resided with them, and to be on familiar terms with them.

There are several superstitious rites and charms performed for the cure of diseases. Water drank out of a certain shell in a certain manner cures the jaundice; and by casting the heart, pouring melted lead *into water* and wearing it. &c.

But as experimental and vital godliness increases, these superstitions will be entirely banished; as a Laird, a short time since, said to one of his tenants the methodist preachers are driving away all the Trows and Bogues and Fairies &c.

Dr. Hibbert states many wonders believed to have transpired

while catching seals in Papa Stour. A person being left all night, accidentally, in a cavern, he held converse with, and heard the lamentations of the seals, who were mermaids in that guise; and one promised if he would restore the skin of her son, she would carry him safe home across the sea. He, therefore, mounted the seal's back, and the seal kept good faith, and brought him to shore; and he was as good as his word to the seal.

Another account is of a man in Unst, who, passing near the sea late at night, surprised some mermaids dancing on the sands; they all fled. He picked up a skin and took it along with him; but he was stopped by a female, quite naked, who requested the skin, as she could not pass to her world without it. But he refused to give it her, and took her home and married her, and had a family by her, who had webbed fingers and toes. She frequently was seen by the sea side conversing with a large seal; and one day a child finding her skin hid in some corn, she ran down to the sea, and put it on, and plunged into the sea to the old seal which was waiting for her. These ridiculous tales are still told in Shetland.

In Unst it was customary to repair to the head of a stream, called Yelaburn, or the burn of health, and to throw, as an acknowledgment to the water Trow, three stones, and then walk round the Pool of Helga Water so many times, silently in the course of the sun, and then take up the water in their hands, and cast it on their heads.

THE RELIGION OF THE ISLANDS, ETC.

The established religion is Presbyterian, which is free from all form and ceremony, and the services are conducted much in the same way as the Dissenters' services in England. There are in all the Islands twenty nine Parishes, twelve regular ministers, and two extra ministers supported by the Royal bounty, and two missionaries. The parishes, ministers, extent, and population, I will give in the following Schedule, which only accounts for twenty three thousand inhabitants, whereas there

Q

are now thirty thousand. The Patron of all the livings is Lord Dundas.

THE PRINCIPAL PARISHES.	MINISTERS.	POPULATION IN 1811.	EXTENT.
Aithsting and Sandsting.	Mr. Jos. Brydon.	1617	Ten miles by six, and two islands, Vementry and Papa Little.
Brassa and Burra Isles.	Mr. G. Hamilton.	1411	Five miles by three, including three other islands, Moss and two Burras.
Delting.	Mr. Patton.	1624	Ten miles by eight, and four islands, Muckle, and Little Roe, Brother Isle, and Fishome.
Dunrossness, Sandwick, Coningscliff and Quarff.	Mr. D. Thompson, Mr. Starkey, & Mr. Garner.	3498	Twenty miles by four, including the Fair Isle and Mousa.
Fetlar and North Yell.	Mr. Watson.	1400	Ten miles by eight.
Lerwick and Gulberwick.	Mr. Barclay.	1949	Eight miles by three.
Nesting and Lunisting.	Mr. M'Gowan.	1866	Four Churches—Nesting, Lunisting, Whalsey, and the Skerries.
North Maven.	Mr. Stephenson.	2024	Sixteen miles by eight, and the isle of Lamma.
Tingwall, Whiteness, and Weesdale.	Mr. Turnbull.	1927	Ten miles by eight; formerly an archdeaconry.
Unst.	Mr. Ingram.	2288	Nine miles by four, and the isle of Uyea.
Walls and Sandness.	Mr. Sinclair.	1882	Nine miles by six, with the isles of Foula and Papa Stour.
South and Mid Yell.	Mr. Robinson.	1434	Eighteen miles by seven, and three islands, Samphra, Hascosea, and Bigra.
Missionaries at South Yell, Whiteness, and Weesdale.	Mr. Elder and Mr. Paterson.	Considerable increase in population since 1811.	

It is evident from the preceding Schedule, and the thinly scattered population, that had the ministers been ever so pious and zealous, they needed more help. Many of the distant islands being only visited yearly, others monthly, &c. Yet considering the size and poverty of the islands, it is as much as they can bear, if not more. The members of the church are examined before they enter, and yearly before they receive the sacrament, and are subject to ecclesiastical censures and punishments, and frequently to the loss of church privileges. The sacrament is given twice a year in Lerwick. On the Friday before the sacrament is the fast-day, when every shop is shut, and every one ceases from work in doors and out; the ships in the harbour are prohibited to send goods on shore, or to take any on board; all are dressed in their sunday clothes, and the church is better filled by far on the fast days, than on the sabbath. They have also the *action* sermon on Saturday, and on Monday after, the thanksgiving service.. The whole of the churches form two Presbyterys and one Synod; and one minister is sent annually to the general assembly in Edinburgh.

Education has greatly progressed within this last century. Brand says that there was not a school, even for the wealthier classes; and complained that the mass of the people were very ignorant.

In 1724, the landholders of the country met and established a school in each parish, obliging the parents to send their children and imposing a heavy penalty if they neglected. Afterwards Education was again neglected. In the present day, however, many Schools are established all over the Islands, but many of them are but ill attended. There are not only parochial Schools, but several connected with The Society for Education in the Highlands and Islands of Scotland. The Schoolmasters in remote parts of the parish catechise the youth on Sunday evenings, and others give an exhortation.

It is said (and I fear often vauntingly) that there is no person in Shetland who cannot read the Bible. But many whom I have exhamined read so unpleasantly and incorrectly, that I can scarcely think it possible for any hearer to be benefitted by such reading.

In giving a view of the character and religious state of the people, I might with propriety say, they are nearly all religious in their own estimation and by profession. They are, generally, a sober, harmless, servile, obsequious, people; but they are far from being free from vice, although there are but few open and avowed sinners, their vices being of a covert and petty character,

Their life is very rural, and in many instances, solitary; but where there are a few cottages together, they are frequently embroiled in litigations and strifes.

They are, generally, addicted to the forms of religion, and a great number are feeling after God, and a good proportion of them are godly persons. Dr. Edmonstone says "The *whole* of the people are respectfully observant of the public duties of religion, and I believe, says he, they may be said to be unaffectedly pious. They were formerly very much attached to their ministers, between whom and themselves there subsisted a degree of parental and filial affection. But the recent innovations of the missionaries have destroyed much of this harmony, and fanaticism, and contempt for the Established Presbyterian church, are now beginning to be openly avowed, and sedulously practised by many. It is (continues the Dr.) truly amusing to observe the progress of this Spiritual revolution, and to witness the folly and inconsistency into which its votaries are led by the extravagance of their leaders. Several of the latter are common fishermen, and bearing the names of some of the apostles, they fancy themselves equally holy and pure, and believe that they are destined to work a similar change on the minds of mankind." This was written concerning the first missionaries, two Independent ministers, sent from Scotland by Mr. Aldine, and some lay teachers they raised up in the Islands. Yet it still stands in his work as a *general* charge against all the missionaries, and shews to the public the enlightened views of Dr. Edmonstone and his friends concerning religion. Now, according to the Dr's opinion, the whole of the inhabitants of these Islands were *formally, externally, universally,* and *really, religious;*—"The whole of the people are respectfully observant of the public duties of religion, and I believe they may be said to be unaffectedly pious;"—and yet he ridicules the idea of their undergoing a change of mind or heart. This he considers fanaticism; or if they are to undergo a change or conversion, it is not to be a similar change to that wrought by the apostles. I dare say Dr. Edmonstone, like many more, supposes the apostles had to convert the nations from systems of paganism &c. to Christianity, and that being done, there needs no more.

I will now give the opinions of two or three individuals, of great weight and authority, in reference to the religious state of the Islands. Brand, who visited Shetland is 1700, says,—" which want of ordinances maketh their case very sad and deplorable; it nurseth ignorance, occasioneth much sin, especially horrid profanation of the Lord's day, by strangers as well as by inhabitants; and doth effectually obstruct the conversion of souls, preaching being the special means of convincing and converting sinners, and building them up in holiness and comfort through faith."— Page 88.

In another place, complaining of their superstitions, he says, " Which obstinacy of these poor deluded souls, persisting in their sin and folly, sheweth the malice and subtilty of that early and grand enemy of man's salvation, labouring to keep some footing in these Islands, if so be his deadly wound might be healed."

Speaking of ignorance, he says, " This black vail draweth the screen round about the soul, whence neither sin, nor misery are felt or seen."

In a work entitled " Thoughts on Orkney and Shetland," of modern date, it is said in reference to religion and education, " A great defect appertains to each of these establishments; namely, that of a clergyman having two or three parishes to attend to, and in some places only one school for two parishes. Common sense, it might be thought, would convince every one, that in such thinly populated Islands, every parish requires a clergyman, and, at least, one school."

About thirty years since, many began to be dissatisfied with their religious experience and privileges, and to desire and seek after something in religion, more *spiritual* and *powerful*, than they, at that time, enjoyed. This was brought about by reading Mr. Wesley's Journals, and they wrote to Dr. Coke for help; but he being about to leave England on his mission, their request was not attended to, and they obtained help from Mr: Aldine, who sent over Mr. Reed and Mr. Nichol. Mr. Reed is the venerable and excellent Independent minister, still living in Lerwick. Mr. Nichol was wrecked and drowned in the Coldstream, returning from his second visit to these islands. There is now an Independent missionary residing in Walls, and several Independent lay-preachers. There is also in Dunrossness a Baptist deacon, who is a native, and preaches to a small congregation.

Wesleyan Methodism was introduced into these islands by John Nicholson, a native of the parish of Delting, on the Mainland; who had received the grace of God, and joined the Methodists, while in the army; and who, returning through ill health to his native air, was induced to exhort his friends and neighbours to flee from the wrath to come, and embrace a free and full salvation through faith in Christ. The persons awakened and brought to a religious concern he endeavoured to keep together. He then wrote to the Conference requesting help, and they directed the Edinburgh district meeting to send one of their ministers to make enquiries on the spot. They selected Dr. M'Allum, a man of rare talents, learning, and piety, who landed in Lerwick in June, 1821. He preached in Lerwick and some other places. His preaching was made a blessing to several, and was much admired. He gained all the information requisite, which was encouraging and satisfactory, but being unable to attend Conference on account of indisposition, he sent a report which was so satisfactory to the Conference, that they immediately appointed the Rev. Messrs. John Roby, and Samuel Dunn, as missionaries to Shetland, which formed a part of the Edinburgh district; and committed the general superintendence of the mission to the late learned and philanthropic, Dr. Adam Clarke, who was that year, for the third time, president of the Conference; and who so fully devoted himself to promote the interest of the mission, that he might emphatically be styled its " Nursing Father." He twice visited the islands, and, had he lived, he promised me to visit them a third time, and had fixed upon the Rev. John Lomas to accompany him.

In the life of Dr, Clarke, page 117, it is said, " The encouraging accounts of the extensive good resulting from the zealous and unwearied exertions of the missionaries, had long excited the deepest interest in the mind of the Doctor; and with it also a desire to visit the Shetland Islands ; in order, not only to see the good, but to secure it, in as far as experience, judgment, and church discipline, could effect it. The manner in which he was received, and his feelings towards the people, you may see—page 189—" Mr. Scott sent us a present of a fine sheep, some ale, porter, and two bottles of whiskey. Miss Henry came to bid us farewell, and brought us a living lamb, several pounds of butter, bottles of milk, and eggs, &c. Many of the people came off the shore with presents of eggs; fish they thought too mean to offer."

" We have now left this very affectionate people," says the Doctor. " Many of them followed the vessel along the shore, till we got to the north entrance of Vaila Sound, and shouted farewell from the shores. It is not likely I shall ever more visit these regions, but I may work for them though I cannot see them."

All, therefore, that could be done by man, the Doctor did to promote the prosperity of this mission. Chapels were built, and preachers' houses ; circuits were formed, and at length six missionaries were regularly appointed, and fourteen or fifteen hundred members were united. The Doctor obtained from his personal friends, for the support of this mission, many princely donations ; from R. Scott, of Penesford, near Bristol, in his life and at his death about £5000.

The congregation in Lerwick, and the society, have been steady and improving ; and a gallery, I am happy to find, is erecting in the Lerwick chapel, which is much needed. There needs in the Lerwick circuit two more chapels ; one at Scalloway, and one at Catfrith, or somewhere in Nesting. Since Dr. Clarke's death, the mission has rather drooped ; but Methodism has a firm hold upon the confidence and affection of the inhabitants in general; and I trust God will shortly again visit these islands with a gracious outpouring of his spirit. However, it is my prayer that Methodism may continue and flourish in these interesting islands, as long as the sun and moon endure. The influence of Methodism in Shetland, upon all ranks and conditions, has been either directly or indirectly felt. Our schools have had their influence upon the young; our preaching and converse have led to numerous conversions; and many have triumphantly passed into glory. The indirect influence has led to an increase of the number of ministers in the establishment, and also more schoolmasters.

It is also affirmed that the theology of the ministers is improving; Calvinism is dying; and though some deny the direct witness of the spirit, yet justification is preached by faith alone, though but few are exhorted to expect it then and there. We may say that zeal is increased, and more and better sermons are now preached than was the case before Methodism came to the Islands.

CONCLUSION.

Orkney and Shetland have always been united in their histories and destinies. I shall be excusable, therefore, if I devote a page to Orkney. Kirkwall, the capital of the Orkneys, is about one hundred and fifteen miles from Lerwick, the capital of Shetland; and the sea between them is rough, conflicting, and dangerous. I shall never forget crossing from Lerwick to Kirkwall, in the Glen-Albin, a glasgow steamer, when the wind was blowing strong from the south-east. The sea rolled high and broke over the packet; the paddles frequently ceasing to act. I then felt the force of the apostle's words " when he longed for the day". Kirkwall is a better town than Lerwick; the streets are more open, regular, and spacious; and the shops are more modern; indeed, I think the plan of the town is better than Lerwick. It is also greatly embellished with St. Magnus' Cathedral, which is really a stately building. It is very long, and something in the shape of a cross, built of a red kind of stone. The windows are large, some round and ornamental; it has a square tower. The inside, for fifty or sixty feet, is lofty and supported by large pillars, very dirty and dilapidated. At the far end it is enclosed with glass; in which part divine service is performed, and is the only established place of worship in the town; in which two ministers officiate: it has chimes.

Not only is the town embellished with the Cathedral, but even the ruins of the Bishops and Earls Palaces give a grandeur and antiquity to the town.

It is also a Royal Borough; made such when visited by James 5th., 1536.

Lerwick, when contrasted with Kirkwall, is more curious, foreign, and compact; it has a better harbour, and the garrison gives it more of a military aspect.

The general appearance of the Islands is much the same. In Shetland the Islands are larger than in Orkney. The largest Island in Orkney, called Pomona, is only about thirty miles long, and from four to ten wide. The Mainland of Shetland is upwards of sixty miles long and the same width. The Island of Yell, the second in Shetland, is upwards of twenty miles long, which is much larger than the second Orkney Island. There are also more Islands in the Shetland groupe. But the land in Orkney is the best, and in the best state of cultivation; the farms are enclosed, and more thickly inhabited.

The spirit and manners of the common people in Shetland are more unique and primitive. In Orkney the inhabitants more resemble the Scotch.

Orkney is better situated, and has the superiority as being the principal seat of municipal authority.

I think persons, from England, or Scotland, visiting these Islands, would find far less to interest in the country, manners, and customs, of Orkney, than Shetland. For in the latter, the scenes are frequently more awfully grand, desolate, vast, solitary, trackless, and wild; and the Scandinavian manners and customs more preserved.

The best way of getting to Shetland, from the west of England is, to take a steamer from Liverpool to Glasgow; from Glasgow to Edinburgh by coach or canal; and from Leith, the port of Edinburgh, there are two good schooners, the Magnus Triol, and the Norna, which are constantly trading between Leith and Lerwick. The distance by sea is about three hundred and fifty miles, and the fare £1. 10s. 0d.—From the east side of England, London and Leith steamers are convenient; or the Ardincaple from Newcastle to Leith. If you wish for less water and more expensive travelling, a letter packet, most weeks, sails from Peterhead to Lerwick, which is only aboout two hundred miles by sea.

www.ingramcontent.com/pod-product-compliance
Lightning Source LLC
LaVergne TN
LVHW081346060426
835508LV00017B/1441